ENDORSEMENTS

"Very few books do I consider 'must reads' for anyone in church leadership, but this is one. Katie Lance takes us into the heart of what has become a deeply divisive issue, but the Holy Spirit brings unity and truth through her words. After reading and re-reading it, I'm still blown away by the courage, honesty, and clarity. I wish I had it to process with others 27 years ago when I started in ministry, but I am convinced and committed to using it now."

—Rev. Santes Beatty,
Director of Next Gen Ministries for The Wesleyan Church

"This book is a must-read for any church leader seeking to build a ministry grounded in holiness and collaboration. Rev. Katie Lance beautifully captures the Spirit's call for men and women to lead *together* in God's kingdom. The next generation is done waiting for the church to get this right. The time is now."

—Rev. Zach Coffin,
Director of Partnership for Kingswood Learn;
Consultant and Coach

"Katie Lance has written a real-life book full of real-life examples of the ungodly, unholy, and at times, almost unbelievable barriers to kingdom ministry that female leaders have experienced at the hands of Christians. This book is a joyful proclamation of the holy power of God to call, equip, and empower both women and men to operate in Spirit-empowered togetherness. Lance provides actionable next steps, habits to practice, and practical ways to catalyze a whole new movement of leaders."

—**Rev. Dr. Christy Lipscomb,**
Lead Pastor of City Life Church, Michigan

"If you limit Katie's writing to 'just another book about men and women in Christian leadership,' you've largely missed her point. We in the church have a distressing tendency to divert our attention and actions away from Jesus' primary calling—love him supremely and love the lost sacrificially. When you read Katie's book, remember that her primary focus is his primary calling.

Katie's passion for Jesus and lost people shines as she beckons us to envision a church that truly influences our world with kingdom fullness—men and women serving Jesus together as his servant leaders, each bringing their stories, strengths, gifts, and perspectives to focus on making and maturing disciples. She invites us with courageous humility—biblically, historically, theologically, and experientially. She encourages us to listen to each other with respect and empathy, treat each other with honor, and walk graciously with Jesus together.

Take Katie seriously. She will stretch you to consider God's church and kingdom ministry in ways that will enlarge our capacity to live out his primary calling. In the end, that's all that really matters."

—**Rev. Dr. Tim Roehl,**
President and Itinerant Multiplier, Fit & Flourish Network

"Katie's book is one full of hope. As she accurately describes the often-discouraging realities of men and women serving as equals within the church, she reminds the reader that nothing is beyond the transforming power of the Holy Spirit. She believes what I hope all will know someday–God calls whom he will, and the Holy Spirit's fire within men and women will not be extinguished! He continues to call both women and men to serve him. Katie provides practical insight and forward guidance as she tackles an essential topic for the church. I recommend this book to pastors and laity alike."

—Rev. Carla Working,
Director of Clergy Care and Development
of The Wesleyan Church

"The vision is simple, but most of us still haven't pulled it off: men and women working together in kingdom fullness. Katie Lance has a way of diagnosing the problem, discerning a solution, and then demonstrating it in real life. In *Live Anointed* Lance turns her lived experience into co-laboring next steps that show a practical way forward beyond mere aspiration."

—Rev. David Drury,
Activator for Global Marketplace Multipliers; Author, Coach

"*Live Anointed* is overflowing with real life experiences and continual references to the Holy Spirit. What a combination! Pastor Katie lifts high the power of learning from the whole range of interactions with people while listening to the Holy Spirit above all – that's the path to Kingdom-Full relationships!"

—Rev. Dr. Wayne Schmidt,
General Superintendent of The Wesleyan Church

"Pastor Katie has laid out one of the substantial problems in the Wesleyan tradition; we have deviated from our core values as described in the first of the General Rules of the Wesleyan Church; "Do no harm." The harm we have caused is that we have disenfranchised half the church from pursuing their calling. Pastor Lance employs one of my favorite techniques for addressing problems. She does not often state her answers to our serious concerns. Rather, she utilizes an ongoing series of questions to reshape the way we view the Church's position. This helps call us all to be part of the solution.

In this book, Rev. Lance will pastorally push you lovingly to hear and experience the heartbeat of the Triune God. This is not principally a book about women in ministry. It's a book about the core meaning of the Gospel and how the Resurrection can radically transform the division created by the fall in the garden of Eden from the garden tomb."

—Dr. Dave Smith,
Professor Emeritus of New Testament and
Biblical Languages, Indiana Wesleyan University

"This remarkable book delves into the crucial process of how the Holy Spirit sanctifies men and women, enabling them to become effective disciples and leaders in the fullness of God's kingdom. It is a clarion call for all ministry leaders to recognize and deploy the gifts of the entire priesthood of believers, fostering a thriving and unified body of Christ.

I wholeheartedly recommend this transformative read to anyone seeking to deepen their faith and understanding of our collective journey towards a Spirit-filled life in Christ. *Live Anointed* will undoubtedly inspire readers to embrace the Holy Spirit's power and lead with purpose, passion, and kingdom fullness."

—Rev. Jervie Windom,
Lead Pastor of Resonate Church, Texas

"God is in the business of the renewal of all things. Katie Lance joins the Holy Spirit as he continues to renew our minds, hearts, and practical responses in joining all God's people to see his kingdom come on earth as it is in heaven. Lance provides a caring and Christ-centered approach to seeing both brothers and sisters working side by side for the kingdom. Do you think prayer is needed? Yes. Are pragmatic actions required? Yes. Are hard conversations essential? Yes. Are we responsible as brothers and sisters to join God in the biblical fullness of the church? Absolutely."

—Rev. Tanya Nace, MA; CEO,
World Hope International (Canada)

"In *Live Anointed*, Pastor Katie Lance offers a profound and timely exploration of how the Spirit empowers all of us to live out our calling as co-laborers in God's kingdom. This book is not just a guide but a rallying cry for men and women in the church to unite in holy love, working together to overcome barriers and fulfill our divine purpose.

Katie's unique perspective, shaped by her dual experience as a caring medical professional and dedicated pastor, brings invaluable insights into church leadership. Through her compassionate and discerning approach, Katie invites us to examine our heart posture toward women in church leadership and to allow the Holy Spirit to lead us in our cooperative efforts.

From tackling the symptoms of dysfunction in Wesleyan/holiness denominations to exploring the divide between belief and practice, this book provides both a critical analysis and a hopeful vision for achieving kingdom fullness. Katie's real-life experiences and examples of ministerial flourishing serve as both encouragement and challenge, urging us to steward our vocations with integrity and passion."

—Dr. Jeannie Trudel,
Vice President of Academic Affairs at Greenville University, Illinois

LIVE
ANOINTED

HOW THE HOLY SPIRIT SANCTIFIES MEN AND WOMEN TO LEAD TOGETHER

LIVE
ANOINTED

HOW THE HOLY SPIRIT SANCTIFIES MEN AND WOMEN TO LEAD TOGETHER

REV. KATIE E. LANCE

WITH BOOK DOULA ELIZABETH GLASS TURNER, M.A.

Live Anointed: How the Holy Spirit Sanctifies Men and Women to Lead Together
Published by Kingdom Fullness Publishing
Okemos, Michigan, U.S.A.

All Scripture quotations, unless otherwise indicated, are taken from the Holy Bible, New International Version®, NIV®. Copyright ©1973, 1978, 1984, 2011 by Biblica, Inc.® Used by permission of Zondervan. All rights reserved worldwide. www.zondervan.com The "NIV" and "New International Version" are trademarks registered in the United States Patent and Trademark Office by Biblica, Inc.®

LANCE, KATIE E., REV., Author
LIVE ANOINTED
KATIE E. LANCE

Library of Congress Control Number: 2024919876

ISBN: 979-8-9912680-0-4, 979-8-9912680-2-8 (paperback)
ISBN: 979-8-9912680-3-5 (hardcover)
ISBN: 979-8-9912680-1-1 (digital)

RELIGION / Christian Ministry / Discipleship
RELIGION / Christian Living / Leadership & Mentoring
RELIGION / Christian Ministry / Pastoral Resources

Writing Coach: Dr. David Drury (DavidDrury.com)
Book Doula: Elizabeth Glass Turner, M.A.
Interior & eBook Design: Amit Dey (amitdey2528@gmail.com)
Publishing Management: Susie Schaefer (finishthebookpublishing.com)

QUANTITY PURCHASES: Schools, companies, professional groups, clubs, and other organizations may qualify for special terms when ordering quantities of this title. For information, email info@kingdomfullness.com

DEDICATION

For Randy, Simon, and Levi,
with all my love.

Doula:

Someone who supports a birthing mother through each stage of labor and delivery through their trained presence, equipping and supporting the mother's decision-making processes and her physical and emotional comfort and well-being.

Dear Elizabeth, my book *doula*,

Embracing my dream from its unseen beginnings, you served me in the knitting-together of this powerful and prophetic gift to the church. Guided by hope and the Holy Spirit, your attentive presence, steadfast patience, wisdom, and creativity breathed life into me and overflowed onto these pages. In the darkest moments you ministered to me, showing me how grieving and lament can be a holy act of worship.

Together, by faith, we delighted in the Lord, witnessing miracles of redemption and sharing in the goodness of God's grace. With exhilarating anticipation and intense birthing pains, we have seen it through to completion. It has been my honor to partner with you; may Jesus be magnified through our obedience.

TABLE OF CONTENTS

FOREWORD I:

Rev. Dr. Ed Love, Executive Director of Church Multiplication and Discipleship for The Wesleyan Church

I have had the privilege of being a friend and mentor of Katie Lance for over a decade. It has been a joy to journey with Katie through the years as she has faithfully pursued her call to ministry. I remember when Katie first shared her call with me and asked me to pray for her as she took her next steps in pursuit of ordination. Because she was fully surrendered to the Lord, I knew God was going to do something special with her life and use her in amazing ways. Through each leadership season, Katie has modeled what it looks like to be a committed disciple maker and leader in the church. I am so grateful Katie and I are currently colleagues in denominational leadership; we work closely together on disciple-making initiatives.

A few years ago, I had an interesting interaction with Katie. She asked me to meet with her to discern a transition point in her ministry. As she shared about her lessons learned in ministry and reflected on how God has used her, I said, "Hold up Katie, I know you look to me as a mentor in your life, but I just want to say, I look up to you! You have grown into a tremendous godly leader and there's no doubt in my mind that God is going to expand your influence." For me, it was a turning point in our relationship where I wouldn't hesitate to call her for a discernment meeting to discuss *my* ministry calling.

Allow me to be honest and vulnerable for a moment. As a male leader, I have always been a bit hesitant to pursue a mentoring relationship with a woman. It may stem from my early ministry training or lack of experience with women in leadership. It may also be because I witnessed a pastor I looked up to fall from grace and give up on his marriage.

At the end of my life, I want nothing more than to hear my Savior say, "Well done, Ed, my good and faithful servant." I desperately want to have a blessed marriage, make it in ministry, and avoid any scandals, which seem to be prevalent these days. However, I have discovered my fears and lack of maturity have caused me to miss out on many life-giving relationships with leaders of the opposite sex. I have learned so much about following Jesus and leading in ministry from Katie and other leaders who are women. At this point, I can't imagine not having the influence of key female voices in my life, and I can't imagine not co-laboring in ministry together with leaders who are women.

The discipleship journey I have been on, which involves what Katie describes as "kingdom fullness" (men and women working together), has caused me to enter deeper levels of spiritual maturity. If I had kept female leaders at a distance, I would not be the leader I am today, and my ministry would not be as blessed as it has been. To be sure, operating with kingdom fullness hasn't been an easy journey, but I don't regret it one bit.

This book, *Live Anointed*, is filled with theological truth and practical wisdom. At different points, the content and stories shared may shock and challenge you. I'd encourage you to continue moving through each chapter listening for the Holy Spirit's voice of truth. The book is designed to create conversations, so I'd encourage you to discuss the content with others and work through your deepest questions.

I believe with all my heart that women and men work better together, and we need each other to sharpen and refine each other. There is a way to have healthy ministry relationships with leaders of the opposite sex. There's no doubt about it, kingdom fullness will require leaders to dig deep into their souls, ask hard questions, and live with accountability. Nevertheless, the kingdom fruit and rewards are worth it!

FOREWORD II:

Rev. Dr. Jo Anne Lyon, General Superintendent Emerita for The Wesleyan Church

Knowing Katie's journey makes this book even more significant. She did not grow up hearing the debates about women in ministry. She grew up hearing all about medical issues with a family of medical professionals. As a result, listening to "table talk," she entered the medical profession herself and for many years served as a successful registered nurse.

Little did Katie and her husband Randy know how radically their lives would be changed when they decided to visit a Wesleyan church one Sunday morning in Lowell, Michigan. They found themselves transformed by the power of God. In a short time, Katie and her husband sensed a call to full-time ministry. They immediately began that journey towards ordination and church planting, leaving behind very successful careers and material possessions. Frankly, as I read the book, I felt as if I were living in Acts 2. Katie completed the ordination requirements over a few years, and they began the journey of church planting and eventually the revitalization of a historic church.

What makes this book so unique are the "surprise barriers" Katie discovered. Yes, barriers to women in ministry. She had never been aware of any of these hidden barriers. This began her journey into scripture and church history, talking with others and being mentored by those who had been in ministry for decades, and engaging with other contributing voices.

Katie articulates these barriers through the heart of one committed to the call of God. As would be typical with a scientific background, Katie simply started with her interviews with pastors (men and women), denominational leaders, and lay people with solid questions to better understand the depth of the problem. She did not approach people with an "axe to grind" but simply asked for reasons in a spirit of humility. Through this approach, she was able to get very honest answers from the hearts of those she interviewed.

Moving forward with this background, she delves into the history of the Wesleyan movement with examples of the vital ministry of women, then onto scripture and theology. Her research is excellent, as noted in the footnotes.

But she does not leave us with history, scripture, and theology only. From this foundation, she gives a pathway to the future with specific action plans to move forward.

This book can be read by one person alone and it would be significant. *But*–the greater impact will be to read this in community with men and women together and to put in practice the thoughtful exercises at the end of each chapter. In so doing, I believe we would see the kingdom of God come on earth *as Jesus imagined and intended.*

Dare we believe this?

CHAPTER ONE

"The Holy Spirit Can't Move
Until You Do"

God is within her; she will not fall. These words are inked into my arm. A casual glance might lead you to assume they're a reminder for me: *God is within me; I will not fall.* That meaning is true, but it's not the reason I bear those words in my skin. I chose these words from Psalm 46:5 as a reminder about the church, the body of Christ: *God is within her; she will not fall.* As part of the fire in my chest that burns with God's calling on my life, I specifically pray for the sanctification of God's church: that together, we are made whole in holy love. Together, we are empowered to resemble Jesus Christ in the ways we love, serve, lead, and live.

How else can men and women thrive together in ministry? Only the Holy Spirit sanctifies us and makes us holy, individually and as a church. No one else has the power to change human hearts. No one else had the power to change mine. When I answered God's call to ministry, I knew God wouldn't ask me to do something that the Holy Spirit wouldn't empower me to obey. It was a costly belief.

It was costly two days after a ministerial training camp, where I received God's call to minister specifically as a lead pastor. When

I came home, a pastor informed me, "I can tell you right now I will not be hiring a woman for this [associate pastor] role. We will be working too closely together." *Holy Spirit, interrupt us.*

It was costly later in pastoral ministry after a challenging gathering where the voices of women were drowned out on sensitive topics. After leaving the difficult meeting, the hurting new pastor I was mentoring practically whispered the words, "So what's the point?" I knew what it was like to feel defeated, to lament; if you're a pastor and a woman, you have to get good at going to the feet of Jesus.

It was costly when someone in leadership said, "You're a great leader, don't become a b*tch." *Holy Spirit, sanctify Your church.*

But then again, when I answered God's call to ministry, I knew God wouldn't ask me to do something that the Holy Spirit wouldn't empower me to obey. It was a beautiful belief. I found something along the road to ministry: God's truth isn't going anywhere, and God is faithful to his promises. The great commission and the great commandment remain our urgent priorities.

It was beautiful when someone who'd been a Baptist elder for thirty years looked at me and asked, "When are you going to accept God's whole calling? The Holy Spirit can't move until you do." When the elder first met me, he didn't support women in pastoral ministry; now, in his words, "the Holy Spirit softened my heart to the truth." He responded by encouraging and exhorting me onward. *God is within her; she will not fall.*

It was beautiful when I'd prayed earnestly over a difficult conversation I was dreading. Mentors prayed alongside me. What I couldn't do on my own, the Holy Spirit did; through hours of prayer, God gave me such compassion. God empowered me to listen deeply, not only to the outer discussion but to the inner voice of the Spirit, prompting and nudging along the way. A hard encounter blossomed into not one but two fruitful discussions with long-term results. *Come, Holy Spirit, come.*

It was beautiful when a group of community pastors from multiple denominations–some of whom had refused to call me by name or include me on the speaking roster–eventually were indignant on my behalf when I was singled out and refused entrance during our group jail visit. It had taken several years of patience for their posture toward me to shift; now, I was one of their own. *Spirit of the living God, make all things new.*

Over the past twelve years of pastoral ministry, God has transformed my life. As the Holy Spirit slowly stretched my understanding of my calling, good-faith leaders who grew and learned alongside me gave me the gift of affirming God's calling on my life. No leader is perfect; that includes me. But God is faithful, and God's grace was busy expanding my vision, just like it was preparing me for ministry before I could have pictured it.

From Scrubs to Sermons

Before I pastored, planted churches, and coached church leaders, I worked as a cardiac medical/surgical and intensive care registered nurse. Nurses see it all (and have been called it all). We know what it is to walk with people through the valley of the shadow of death. We are not easily shocked or embarrassed. My time as a nurse was the best preparation for pastoral leadership that I could've asked for. Sometimes the roles still blend if a church member doesn't have anyone else to change the dressing on their wound.

Many times on my vocational journey, I yearned for God to lay out my entire path, clear as day; an audible voice or maybe a billboard would be nice. But God knew I might bolt if I saw too much of the road ahead of me. Instead, the next step often appeared naturally as God developed a role or skill in the process. As I kept my eyes on Jesus, not the path itself, suddenly, I'd see fruit from what I was doing. In these moments, I realized in new ways that when God calls and I obey, through the power of the Holy Spirit, I am capable. Through the transforming grace of God, "Perfect love drives out fear." (1 John 4:18) [1]

In this way, the Holy Spirit led me step by step on a journey of ministerial study and co-pastoring. Then, the Spirit opened the next steps into a lead pastor role as a church planter. Then, the Holy Spirit opened my next "yes" to God through the opportunity to minister by coaching and training other leaders across denominations.

Bearing Witness

Each step I took felt like a simple matter of obedience; I had to seek God's kingdom. I couldn't outrun James 4:17: "If anyone, then, knows the good they ought to do and doesn't do it, it is sin for them."

Yet even with the discernment and support of mentors, my frustration grew each step of the way as I tried to follow God's call. I encountered hurdles and barriers to growth in ministry—many within my denomination,[2] some beyond it. I was heartbroken, but I also lamented every time I found myself bearing witness to the frustration, uncertainty, anger, and grief of men and women I worked with, coached, or interviewed. I longed for women and men to thrive together in ministry, and I grieved for the body of Christ.

God is within her; she will not fall. These words reassure me when my nurse's ears listen intently to the heartbeat of the body of Christ and hear that all is not well. Through hundreds of hours of interviews, I have listened to the voices of men and women in leadership, including laity, staff pastors, ministry students, lead pastors, leaders of interdenominational organizations, and leaders from different denominations. In this book, you will encounter some of their stories.

Before I started this project, I spent time in many settings just sitting with my brothers in a posture of learning, present in the moment to listen without reply, justification, or representation; just listening to my brother and the Holy Spirit. The prevailing church culture across multiple denominations became evident when so many leaders I spoke with felt it prudent to remain anonymous out of concern over retaliation from their church leaders and authority figures. There was real concern over being "canceled" in collegiate relationships and formal partnerships or even putting livelihoods at risk. In the examples I share, names or defining details are changed. My prayer is that readers are not distracted by "who" a subject is, but rather that together we can lean in and listen to the Holy Spirit's message.

Meanwhile, as I write this, three pastors I know have left ministry because they're exhausted from wasting energy fighting just to participate in conversations, professional settings, and decision-making; they are women. During that same time, four others transferred to different denominations from the ones they were previously pastoring in. Ministry is hard enough in itself for all pastors; these women didn't enter ministry dreaming of spending so much time navigating unending challenges resulting from the fact they are women.

Yet with all this happening, the great commission continues to call us all. We need all of us, men and women together, leading with joy and holy conviction so we can reach a hurting world for Jesus. The challenges in front of us are not all-powerful; God is. The Holy Spirit calls us to work side by side, like our Creator intended when walking with Adam and Eve together in "the cool of the evening;" like Jesus welcoming Mary to sit and learn from his teaching alongside other disciples; like men and women gathering in prayer together on the day of Pentecost.

Burdened for Kingdom Fullness

The idea of kingdom fullness paints a picture of God's design for the body of Christ. Leadership in The Wesleyan Church shares a vision of unleashing a "kingdom force." For the church to be whole, functioning, and mobilized, this kingdom force is "kingdom full." What is kingdom fullness?

Kingdom fullness celebrates that all believers, filled with the Holy Spirit, are empowered and equipped to build up the church in any and every way according to the gifting and calling of the Holy Spirit. Kingdom fullness represents a force of men and women, lay and clergy; it is multi-ethnic, multi-socioeconomic, multi-generational; with everyone engaged in ministry together.

We encounter this fullness in Acts 2:17-21. Citing Joel 2:28-32, "In the last days, God says, "I will pour out my Spirit on all people. Your sons and daughters will prophesy, your young men will see visions, your old men will dream dreams. Even on my servants, both men and women, I will pour out my Spirit in those days, and they will prophesy. And everyone who calls on the name of the Lord will be saved." The Holy Spirit empowers us to live together in vibrant fullness. But what is our current posture toward the Holy Spirit?

"Those of us who heard her preach, last year, at Lodi, where she held the almost breathless attention of five thousand people, by the eloquence of the Holy Ghost, know well where is the hiding of her power."[3]
—Thomas K. Doty on Rev. Julia A.J. Foote, 1879

Worth It

Do we still believe in sanctification? Do we trust the scriptural witness to the transforming grace of God? We already affirm that God's saving grace rescues us from the toll of brokenness and self-centered sinfulness when we place our trust in Jesus Christ and by faith are justified, receiving new life. But across centuries, using different descriptions or terms, many Christians also affirm the power of God's transforming grace now, in this life. It shapes our love and empowers our actions to be more and more like Jesus. In the broad Wesleyan Methodist tradition of the Christian faith, we may describe this deeper work of God's transforming grace as sanctification or holiness or being made complete or perfect in holy love. It is the ever-deepening journey of being made holy until that glorious day we arrive home in heaven. Whatever words are used, in the Wesleyan/holiness tradition, we don't stop at faith in Jesus Christ which puts us back in alignment with God. We celebrate that when we receive the Holy Spirit, the Holy Spirit empowers us to be more and more Christlike: sanctified, made holy, and characterized by holy love.

"Sisters, shall not you and I unite with the heavenly host in the grand chorus? If so, you will not let what man may say or do, keep you from doing the will of the Lord or using the gifts you have for the good of others. How much easier to bear the reproach of men than to live at a distance from God. Be not kept in bondage by those who say, 'We suffer not a woman to teach,' thus quoting Paul's words, but not rightly applying them."[4] –Rev. Julia A.J. Foote, 1879

If we believe in sanctification, we believe in the promise of holiness lived out together in community, "so that the body of Christ may be built up." In human strength, this is impossible; "but with God, all things are possible." (Matt. 19:26) That doesn't mean it's easy, or pretty, or comfortable. It means it's worth it.

The church is worth it.

Church leaders are worth it: our spiritual brothers and sisters are worth having difficult conversations. They are worth our time and the effort to sit and listen to their challenges, concerns, grief, and sometimes, their holy anger—anger, the often-misunderstood secondary emotional response to your own initial emotion of hurt, fear, or grief.

Learning discernment is also worth it. Sometimes practicing discernment looks like listening to the hard-won wisdom of mentors; sometimes, it means setting aside the "conventional wisdom" of others. There are times when well-intended advice doesn't align with the conviction of the Holy Spirit, steeped in the Word of God. At times, I've had to release comments I've received, like:

- "This is too deep a problem to get anywhere, I suggest you die on another hill."
- "If you're going to kick a hornet nest you'll get the stinger."
- "Go with the goers, don't try to change people's minds."
- "Things have come a long way for women in the church, I know two female lead pastors now, what's the problem?"
- "This isn't something that can be addressed effectively corporately, it would be more realistic in your local church context."

Even if pastors, church leaders, and God's church are worth it, though—why labor over this book? Is this effort worth it? There are already fantastic resources available by women in pastoral leadership. As you explore kingdom fullness, I encourage you to explore writing from pastors like Rev. Tara Beth Leach in *Empowered*, Dr. Carolyn Moore in *When Women Lead*, Rev. Danielle Strickland and Bob Goff in *Better Together*, Nancy Beach in *Gifted to Lead: The Art of Leading as a Woman in the Church* and Rev. Kadi Cole in *Developing Female Leaders*. Plenty of work has also been done on the biblical theology of women in pastoral ministry and church leadership, including the scholarship of Dr. Ken Schenck in the booklet *Why Wesleyans Favor Women in Ministry* and the writings of Methodist New Testament scholar Dr. Ben Witherington III.

Alongside the great resources already available, I've labored over this book because God tucked it away in my heart and would not let me dodge it. From a practical perspective, I pray this book is a dog-eared, useful, encouraging guide for how men and women can thrive together in ministry.

To that end, this book is *not*:

- Another deep-dive biblical and theological defense of women at all levels of church leadership or another defense of egalitarian marriage dynamics (many resources are already available on those topics)

- A sociological examination of women in the workplace (though the findings discussed in this book are informed by hundreds of interviews)

- A book-length rant against men

- An ongoing complaint that doesn't offer practical tools, solutions, or positive examples of vocational flourishing

- A resource with examples solely drawn from one denomination or solely relevant to one denomination

- A memoir exploring only my personal experiences

Instead, this book highlights the challenges and hope that echo through testimonies and perspectives shared by over 150 pastors and district and denominational leaders: women and men, unnamed and named, current and former. The dynamics explored in this book are informed by interviews and coaching encounters with clergy from The Church of the Nazarene, Assemblies of God, The United Methodist Church, The Wesleyan Church, The Free Methodist Church USA, Congregational churches, the Church of God (Anderson), non-denominational churches, and even The Christian Reformed Church. This is a multi-denominational book shaped by pastors in multiple Christian bodies, most Wesleyan/holiness or Wesleyan/Methodist.

In particular, we will explore:

- Symptoms of dysfunction in the body of Christ in its expression in Wesleyan/holiness denominations, through a North American lens
- The divide between stated belief and lived values in everyday practice
- Perspectives from both women and men as the church identifies barriers to kingdom fullness
- "Wins" and examples of ministerial flourishing
- Hurdles that hinder vocational discernment and leadership development
- Practical tools for pursuing kingdom fullness at local levels
- An anointed vision for healthy kingdom fullness

I pray the Holy Spirit meets you wherever you are, ministers to your soul, and allows the time you spend in this book to be worth it.

Wound Care

The Holy Spirit is calling men and women who are willing to step into these conversations with boldness, grace, compassion, and uncompromising grit to see it through. We have opportunities to steward space for unrushed, Spirit-guided dialogue.

As I interviewed brothers from multiple denominations working in senior leadership at local church and organizational levels, I listened to their experiences as they shared what they were taught formally and through modeling about working with women. I heard their fears, concerns, and frustration. In every conversation, without exception, when I was invited to reciprocate–to share my story and the current barriers to men and women thriving together in ministry–I heard, "I had no idea" or "You're telling me things I have never heard before."

The purpose, then, of sharing this content is to address this gap and inform our practices so that we can examine how we can flourish together co-laboring for the Kingdom. As Courtney Dunn noted in an article on Sacred Alliance, a website sponsored by Wesley Seminary, "If we truly want to begin to understand how churches can go about changing the culture toward women preachers, we must tell the stories of women preachers. Through these stories, we begin to understand the culture that surrounds the pulpit." [5]

For many people, both women and men, this topic is deeply personal. This discussion can bring to the surface a variety of responses. To enter this conversation well, it's helpful to engage with prayer, humility, and sensitivity. In reading, if you experience anger, grief, uncertainty, conviction, or other strong reactions, I encourage you to notice those responses, pause, and pray. If you need to, set aside this book until the Lord calls you to return to reading. I also encourage you to read it alongside someone else or in conversation with a group.

If we have not heard each other through the unity of the Holy Spirit, then God is calling us to hear the testimonies of anointed women. God is calling us to honor the good-faith questions and concerns of honest men.

In this space, the Holy Spirit is inviting you, whoever you are, to bring your hopes, hurts, misunderstandings, and missed moments to the feet of Jesus. "There is one body and one Spirit, just as you were called to one hope when you were called; one Lord, one faith, one baptism; one God and Father of all, who is over all and through all and in all" (Ephesians 4:4-6).

God has drawn my heart closer to him in the process of developing this resource. I especially want to mention gratitude to my brothers in Christ who have invested in me, encouraged me, and supported me along the way; as I started the book writing process, one said, "call me when things get tough. I'm cheering you on!"

I invite you to pray every time you open this book. With you, I am asking the Holy Spirit to, "search me, God, and know my heart; test me and know my anxious thoughts. See if there is any offensive way in me, and lead me in the way everlasting" (Psalm 139:23-24). With you, I pray God will continue to convict us, empower us, heal us, encourage us, sanctify us, and unite us. Only the Holy Spirit can anoint us to pursue the kingdom of God and tune our hearts to align with his.

Will you pray with me for God's grace to quiet our assumptions and stir our hearts, so women and men may thrive together in new ways as we partner to reach the lost and glorify God? Through the testimonies in these pages, I pray you will find fresh hope for a holy, renewed body of Christ.

I also pray that:

- Women will receive and visualize their full calling from God with support to step into that calling.

- Men will visualize a kingdom-full team and will carry the burden for equipping women and men to thrive together as we live the great commission.
- Denominations will gain new longing for their leadership landscape to reflect anointed kingdom fullness.
- Every denomination will discern and pursue the next steps toward kingdom fullness at all levels of leadership.
- Ordained women will be appointed without needing to look outside their home denominations for ministerial positions.

When the Holy Spirit poured out on the day of Pentecost, all believers received the empowered gift of the Holy Spirit. All believers, who were all in, sent all over the world. I am believing God for his dream for the church. I am believing God for restoration. I am believing God for a fresh anointing on his church, his body.

God is within her; she will not fall.

Chapter One Reflection & Discussion Questions

By Elizabeth Glass Turner, M.A., Editor and Writer, Former Pastor and Campus Minister

Pastor Katie relates a story of a gentleman who told her, "the Holy Spirit can't move until you do." She has a medical background and knows the tension between the need to take action to intervene for critical patients alongside the reality of the importance of prayer, for instance.

In the Wesleyan Methodist branch of the Christian faith, we celebrate the ongoing activity of the Holy Spirit in the lives of believers; we also affirm that God gives us the freedom to accept or reject prompts of grace. This means God doesn't want us to stay sedentary; the Holy Spirit prods the body of Christ, urging us to act because we will find grace in the taking of action—not in wandering up to watch God's activity like it's a spectator sport, popcorn in hand. God will not force any individual—or any expression of the body of Christ—where it refuses to go.

As you reflect on this opening section, watch for two things: ways the Holy Spirit is prodding you to move, and ways the Holy Spirit might be prodding your congregation, cohort, region, conference, or tradition to move. "The Holy Spirit can't move until you do."

Discussion Questions

1. *Pastor Katie describes some costs as she follows her call to ministry. Did any of those examples surprise you? Did any of her "beautiful" moments surprise you? If so, why?*

2. *Pastor Katie mentions working as a registered nurse before becoming a pastor. Do you know bi-vocational pastors or those who entered ministry already established in a career?*

3. *If you're familiar with initiatives like "Marketplace Multipliers" in The Wesleyan Church, how might bi-vocational or second-career pastoral ministry be distinct from engaging in the "marketplace" through the witness all Christians are called to?*

4. *As the call to ministry unfolded in Pastor Katie's life, she mentions, "the next step often appeared naturally" as her gifts were developed along the way. How have you experienced God leading in your life?*

5. *Are you familiar with the term "sanctification"? What associations or meaning comes to mind when you hear it?*

6. *Pastor Katie mentions interviewing pastors from a variety of denominations. If you grew up going to church, what is your denominational background? If you grew up going to nondenominational churches, do you know what theological background you grew up with?*

7. *The New Testament is full of examples of "kingdom fullness" —people from different backgrounds encountering the power of Jesus Christ and the anointing of the Holy Spirit. How do you see your role in God's kingdom? Is God asking you to surrender your idea of what your role should be?*

This Week

Take ten minutes today to pray for pastors' spouses and other church leaders, volunteers, pastors, and anyone discerning a possible call to pastoral ministry.

CHAPTER TWO

Diagnosing the Body

"These people are not drunk, as you suppose. It's only nine in the morning! No, this is what was spoken by the prophet Joel: 'In the last days, God says, I will pour out my Spirit on all people. Your sons and daughters will prophesy, your young men will see visions, your old men will dream dreams. Even on my servants, both men and women, I will pour out my Spirit in those days, and they will prophesy'"
(Acts 2:15-18).

One of my favorite things to do as a nurse was taking a patient's vital signs. In acute care, I encountered many heart patients. I loved the moment when I slid my stethoscope on, put a hand on a patient's chest, and listened deeply—an action called "auscultation" in medical terms. As a nurse, I had to learn the discipline of listening well. After I became a lead pastor, I was thrilled to see Dr. Tim Roehl specifically naming this kind of close listening in his book *Lead by Listening.*

We all can learn a lot by listening well. One reason I loved those moments hearing the rub-dub of a patient's heart. I could listen and offer a silent prayer for them. In medicine, you encounter people who are broken in many different ways.

This was something I learned at an early age, my parents and stepparents serving their communities as homemakers, doctors, dentists, and nurses. I grew up before HIPPA patient confidentiality rules entered American healthcare. I went to work with my parents: I made cookies with Jesse in the hospital kitchen, sorted paperclips and brought water to patients in their rooms, swiveled in the chair at the emergency room desk, and had secret handshakes with the ambulance drivers when they brought in patients. Dr. Myrtle even pulled my first tooth on the gurney in triage room three. I helped transport X-rays from the radiology department, carrying the two-foot by three-foot sheets of plastic in manilla envelopes with handwritten notes on them. I watched my parents' "bedside manner" in hospital rooms and chairside in the dental office. I watched them care for people in their most vulnerable times and lovingly lead them through. I watched my mother hold the hands of dying people and weep with families in their loss. I watched them care for broken bodies and broken people.

Every day, medical professionals meet people trying to ignore symptoms like fatigue, an achy shoulder, and heartburn: some of those people will learn they have serious blockages and dysfunction in their hearts. Doctors learn to discern between conditions like acid reflux and a heart attack when they listen to the heart, run blood work, order tests, and review imaging.

Doctors and nurses know *diagnosis requires discernment and discernment requires paying attention.* A lot of conditions are caught—or slip through the cracks—depending on a physician's ability and willingness to listen to a patient. How much more is this true when the Holy Spirit convicts us to pay attention to the body of Christ, the church? How much more is this true in the spiritual sense, not just the physical?

You and I don't have the luxury of running an MRI on the church. Yet God hasn't left us empty-handed: through the empowerment of the Holy Spirit and the conviction of the Word of God, we see the ways the body of Christ can break down—as well as "the most excellent way" forward (I Cor. 12:31b).

Discernment is possible through careful listening. This is true when a nurse or doctor listens to a patient's heart. It's also true when followers of Jesus listen to the Holy Spirit through the Word of God and when we listen and truly hear our brothers and sisters in Christ. We learn about the body of Christ when we listen to the body in more ways than one.

Hurdles to Discernment: Listening Behind "I'm Fine"

If you ask an emergency room nurse how they'd respond to a farmer who says, "I'm fine," they'll probably laugh. In hospitals, if a farmer comes in with a complaint, it's probably already urgent. Someone is likely quietly sounding an alarm. Farmers can have a terrible wound or injury and still insist on finishing a field before reluctantly arriving for medical attention.

There are a lot of reasons we say, "I'm fine" when we are not. Sometimes we're busy and don't want to be interrupted or waste time. Sometimes we avoid interactions we're embarrassed to admit are still deeply uncomfortable: even adults avoid doctors, nurses, and hospital hallways. And sometimes, we say, "I'm fine" because of distrust or discomfort disclosing the actual level of pain.

It's not unusual to encounter patients who have been ignoring their woundedness. Frequently, patients are admitted to hospitals for sepsis (systemic infection) originating from a single location of infection; legs and feet are especially vulnerable.

One time, a patient I'll call Ellen arrived at the hospital months after nicking the skin on her toe. An infection had settled in, and the wound festered, so she kept it covered constantly. For months, she didn't take off her sock or shoe, limping in pain before she finally sought help. She was terrified of going to the hospital, being admitted, and potential interventions like surgery. She was overwhelmed by the financial costs of a hospital stay or medications. She knew the pain of the present but feared the pain of the unknown.

Some wounds hit your nose before they meet your eyes. My senses were introduced to her wound down the hallway, long before I saw the patient. Cutting off her sock, a massive wound was revealed, spreading from her toe up into her leg. It was so deep the bone was visible, and we immediately started her on multiple antibiotics. She needed surgery and spent weeks in the hospital. The infection that started with a tiny cut on her toe almost killed her. I took care of many patients in similar situations who didn't have the same outcome; their infected wounds were too much for their bodies, and they didn't survive.

It's easy to ignore our wounds or try to keep them covered up. Over fifteen years of ministry, I've walked with hundreds of church leaders—men and women—who entrusted me with their concerns, experiences, and pain. In my own experiences, it took time, reflection, and community for me to acknowledge that some comments and interactions I experienced as a pastor just weren't okay. I wanted to believe the best of others, to assume that behind the words, "the heart" was in the right place. And sometimes, it was; sometimes wounds are unintentional, or a good-faith pastor simply isn't sure how best to handle an interaction. At the same time, it's easy to reframe conversations in a way that minimizes problems, because (for a while) it allows us to just keep going. It's fine. No really, it's fine.

Sisters and brothers, we are not fine. Pastors who are men aren't fine. Pastors who are women aren't fine. And if you know a pastor who's a woman, it's safe to assume she's experienced far more than she has felt safe expressing, sometimes even to herself.

Discernment: Leaning In Toward the Wound

Healing is impossible if a doctor shrinks away from an injury, standing arms-length away, eyes averted. As much as a patient must allow a nurse or doctor to lift a homemade bandage to see beneath, physicians also must be able to calmly, tenderly, lean in toward the wound. Only when we see what's underneath can cleaning, examination, and treatment begin.

Over the coming chapters, we will look together beneath the bandage, as interviews, statistics, and testimonies give shape to both injury and recovery. My prayer is that as apprentices to the Great Physician, the Kind Healer, we also will pray for grace to calmly, tenderly lean in, honest and unflinching.

In doing so, we're not examining the wound of vocational hurdles to the exclusion of other vocational injuries; all pastors get "sheep bite," as the saying goes. Ministry is hard, period. It's beautiful and rewarding, too, but any church leader can tell you of brutal challenges and hard seasons. Church leaders were burning out before COVID-19, before grieving the death of George Floyd, before profound political upheaval, before a quick series of high-profile ministerial scandals across denominations in the United States.

Ministry is challenging for every pastor.

Yet whether I speak with women just beginning to follow God's call into pastoral ministry or women who have led in the church for years, most have similar kinds of stories. I have my own. Usually, it took time to acknowledge what was happening. Many times, I looked past problematic comments or mistreatment, because I truly believed the heart it was coming from was sincere and unaware of its impact. Other times, I was uncertain whether addressing hurdles would be worth the hassle or possible negative repercussions on relationships I genuinely valued.

A couple of years ago as I chatted with a dear friend and colleague, he commented, "Overall, I think things are looking much better for women in ministry, pretty great actually." I answered, "With respect, I disagree with you. I think women in ministry are worse off than ten years ago." I shared a few examples.

According to 2024 data from my denomination, The Wesleyan Church, 23% of credentialed pastors are women. This figure includes ministerial students, retired pastors, and pastors on reserve or unappointed. In 2024, credentialed women comprise just 3% of lead or co-pastors. In 2022, no ordained clergywomen were elected to our General Board, the highest governing board of my denomination. Of twenty-two district superintendents in North America, none were women.

In the past year, I spoke with a colleague who participated on a board a decade ago to discuss women in leadership. I asked her what came of it. She shrugged her shoulders and sighed, "we're still here discussing the same problem today."

I have spoken with multiple men from both complementarian and egalitarian denominations who have initiated conversation to tell me their daughter or granddaughter feels a call to ministry and asking what to do because they don't see hope for their loved ones to find a place in their denominational structure beyond children's, women's or worship ministries. Brothers in Christ have wept and grieved next to me, lamenting for the church, for their denominations, for the tension, for losing hope. Denominations that support women's ordination need to wake up and put our actions and advocacy where our official stance is.

Women who prepare for ministry frequently struggle to find work in pastoral ministry in congregations, especially in denominations with congregational forms of church government, in which local churches elect pastors. One time, a church leader told me that hiring a woman "just wasn't worth the risk" to their marriage and church: "I can't work alone with a woman responsibly." But that response wasn't unique to me; at least ten different pastors who are women have shared nearly identical experiences with me. All of them belong to denominations that officially support women in lead ministry roles.

Maybe you've heard statements from church leaders like some of the following comments I've received in conversations or heard in conference settings. Maybe you haven't heard these comments, you've made them. If you have, please know women in church leadership appreciate that you're taking the time to read this, and I hope you'll continue through the discomfort. During my time in local church and coaching ministry, I've heard comments like:

- "It's not responsible of me as a lead pastor or safe for me as a husband to be working that closely with women."

- "I believe in women in ministry, but in my church, this model of all-male leadership is what works for us."

- "It's safe for me to work with her because she's like my granddaughter, I raised her through youth group."

- "I don't have a problem with hiring a female pastor, but our board is not interested in interviewing female candidates."

- "What will happen if her children are sick on a Sunday morning? How will she preach?

This kind of reasoning—this kind of theology—is flawed whether deployed about pastors who are women *or* pastors who are men. The hurdle appears when, organizationally and individually, leaders expect women called into pastoral ministry to be the exception, not the norm. If you believe a woman in church leadership is the exception, you don't see the absence of women as a deficiency, a problem, or even something to grieve. If women are exceptions, low numbers are inevitable.

Of course, to believe women are an exception is to ignore the truth of Pentecost. At Pentecost, the Holy Spirit poured out on women and men gathered together praying in the upper room. Women in church leadership aren't an exception; we've been here from the beginning.

And since the birth of the church, ministry has been challenging for every pastor. Today, women simply have additional hurdles on top of the usual difficulties (and that's true for any denomination). Many ministers know the whiplash of the unexpected: men and women alike are familiar with sudden conversational pivots, shifting from navigating something substantive to fielding petty criticism like comments on our appearance, age, or clothing.

Celebrating Champions of Kingdom Fullness:
The late Rev. Wayne Wright co-pastored and taught with
his wife, the late Virginia Wright, who pursued graduate
studies in theology. Married in 1949, they spent their lives
ministering in the U.S. and around the globe. Rev. Wright
served as General Secretary with Wesleyan World Mis-
sions for The Wesleyan Church. One pastor remembers
Rev. Wright commenting on her and the handful of women
in an ordination course. "Ministry will require sacrifices

from all of you. But gentlemen, these women in the room with you will pay a higher price. And there will be something special in their ministry because of it." In 2015, the Wrights passed away within six weeks of each other.

Some of the most minor hassles I've experienced as a woman in pastoral ministry fall in this category. Sometimes, you can't win: I've been criticized when I wore a skirt, then later criticized when I wore a pantsuit ("Are you trying to act like a man, wearing a pantsuit?"). I've been told my lipstick was too bright. After one worship service when the Holy Spirit was present and people surrendered their lives to Christ, one man's response was to comment on my hair. Surely the Holy Spirit groaned a bit that day at the way the man missed the kingdom activity right in front of him; I know I did. Unfortunately, those kinds of comments are common for many leaders in visible positions, pastors included.

But there are harder comments from church members, too. One day as I greeted people at my new church, someone looked me in the eye and said, "You will never be my pastor; I will never respect you; and I will never listen to you preach." It was said because I'm a woman. But comments from laypeople aren't the most problematic.

One pastor preparing to launch a church plant found herself in a meeting with a supervising leader. The leader said, "Well, show us your plan...and don't tell us it includes another baby on the way. We know how that slows things down!" As it turned out, she did launch a new church plant; and did so shortly after giving birth. She was convicted to follow God's call to church planting, and she followed through on it. But she had to shut out these kinds of demoralizing, intrusive comments and verbalized doubt about family and ministry compatibility in general.

Many men also faithfully engage as dedicated fathers, up with newborns while pastoring churches or working in the secular workforce. At times, pastors who are parents encounter some remarkable resistance from church leaders and lay members alike. I've encountered anecdotes from dads pastoring in denominations with higher percentages of pastors who are women; sometimes in these settings, men encounter hurdles and criticism when they seek schedule flexibility or the paternity leave offered by their denominations.

Comments like those directed at the church planter are unprofessional and demonstrate insensitivity (many couples have endured miscarriage or fertility challenges). These comments also assume roles and childcare are carried out in a very narrow, specific way in someone else's household; they reveal a not-so-subtle perspective on whether women can be caring mothers while working outside the house.

Meanwhile, unmarried pastors—men and women alike—handle multiple challenges, handling intrusive questions about relationship prospects while managing a tough financial landscape: a 2018 study in one Wesleyan/holiness denomination found that two-thirds of pastors in that denomination couldn't live on their pastoral salary alone.[1] Often, women who are called to pastoral ministry after working in more equitable settings are especially stunned at unprofessional commentary on relationships or parenting status. In many workplace contexts, commentary like this gives human resource directors pounding migraines.

In a different instance, another minister with decades of pastoral experience was being considered for an executive leadership role in her holiness denomination. At the denomination's conference, before voting took place, a man approached a microphone to ask if the church leader been through menopause yet and if she was "hormonally stable." A private, personal, and irrelevant medical matter became a topic for dissection and deliberation in a large group. The very fact the question was brought up cast doubt on her inherent reliability and leadership capability. Was she expected to give details on this personal subject? Did she need to defend her God-given body? Or was the question aimed to embarrass, humiliate, or catch off-guard? If she *had* reacted with shock or anger, her reaction itself would've been used as evidence she wasn't "stable." Men under consideration for high-level church leadership roles generally aren't asked personal questions about their reproductive systems, hormonal state, or other intrusive medical information like blood sugar numbers or dementia family history.

Inappropriate or unprofessional questions and remarks are a frustrating gauntlet to navigate graciously, especially when they are on the spot. But even the most jaw-dropping comments aren't as tricky to handle as other hurdles. These challenges range from hostile ministers in your community to hurdles to ministerial training, to one-size-fits-all statements on who is eligible for some roles.

Criticism of my clothes is minor compared to a local congregation praying my church will close since I am "leading it in sin" because I'm a woman (that happened). Comments on my hair are minor compared to a woman being told she'll never be considered for an associate role because she's a woman (that too). And saying a woman will never be considered for a position is just a portion of the heartbreak my sisters who are women of color hear when they try to follow God's call (God's heart is breaking).

Every time experiences like these are dismissed for the sake of ease or the status quo, women have to choose how quickly to entrust a male colleague the next time one asks, "so, how are things going?" Some men in church leadership still respond with skepticism to experiences like these. If one of my brothers doesn't want to express doubt openly about what their sisters are disclosing, hesitation usually turns toward the interpretation of events or whether their sister's response is proportionate: "she's oversensitive," or "I'm sure he didn't mean anything by it," or "that's just my sense of humor," or "she just makes everything about gender."

But how can we exercise discernment if we only hear part of the truth because we wave away or dismiss the uncomfortable parts? Denying a knee injury doesn't help it heal; trying to run on an injured knee makes the injury worse. Ignoring problems in the body may seem best in the short run, but it shortchanges the promises of Christ, the call of scripture, and the empowering transformation of the Holy Spirit.

This doesn't mean women shouldn't ever be critiqued as leaders; it doesn't mean every struggle endured by pastors who are women is due to their sex. We're simply acknowledging that for a variety of reasons, sometimes our brothers in leadership hesitate to trust the sense and discernment of their sisters in Christ. And it means the body of Christ needs women and men in leadership together, discerning together.

These are just a few of the symptoms we need to hear, believe, and sit with before we can begin to live more authentically into kingdom fullness. This is part of the reality of the wound we're facing. The question is whether we will take a deep breath and lean in.

In the chapters ahead, we'll hear more from many leaders. Some are able to speak freely; others are vulnerable. The voices of women and men are both essential, individually and together.

God has given us everything we need to pursue the great commission. You and I will answer to God for how we stewarded the calling and vocation of others; we will answer for how we steward our influence, our power, and our leadership. I cannot stand before God and try to tell him I didn't know better or that I didn't have what I needed. As we read in the second epistle of Peter, "his divine power has given us everything we need for a godly life through our knowledge of him who called us by his own glory and goodness" (2 Peter 1:3).

By the power of the Holy Spirit, through the inspiration of scripture and the body of Christ that sharpens us in community, we have what we need. Through the testimony of others, we are hearing what we need to hear—which means we're responsible for listening to what we've heard, learning from it, and acting on it. You and I have what we need to discern the truth and implement kingdom fullness in our leadership.

Sisters and brothers, we are not "fine." We're not okay. The body is limping. But the Great Physician is leaning in to heal and restore holiness and wholeness. "See, I am doing a new thing! Now it springs up; do you not perceive it? I am making a way in the wilderness and streams in the wasteland" (Isaiah 43:19).

Come, Holy Spirit. Empower us to discern Your work.

Chapter Two Reflection & Discussion Questions

By Pastor Jordan Loman, Co-Planter and Co-Lead Pastor of Emmaus Church, NC

Two chapters in, you have read enough that you may feel some tension. Though this topic can sometimes raise heart rates, the purpose of this conversation is not to push you to choose a side or elicit an emotive response.

As I write this, I reflect on the last eight years spent church planting and co-pastoring alongside my husband. There were times my role and title were undermined, times I was excluded from district-initiated meetings. For the most part, I learned to live around it, the way some of you may have learned to live with chronic pain. As much as a chronic condition hinders everyday activities, it can easily begin to become part of your identity. I have my experiences; my brothers and sisters have theirs. Ultimately, our response cannot be to choose sides to defend. These chapters provide stories of the consequences that occur when we choose a side and the wounding impact it has on brothers and sisters whose hearts have not had the opportunity to be heard.

Brothers and sisters, as a means of grace, the Lord provides spaces of genuine communication and heartfelt sharing. May we come back to scripture and sit with truth, not dismissing our experience but, in the tension, allowing truth in Christ to lead us forward in healing and partnership. I invite you to take a breath and pray as you prepare your heart to discuss this chapter further.

(Inhale)	*(Exhale)*
Abba Father,	*provide peace,*
Prince of Peace,	*pour out Your Spirit,*
Holy Spirit,	*bring unity.*

Discussion Questions

1. *Have you heard the phrase "hurt people hurt people"? Whatever your role in church or ministry, take a few minutes to let yourself recall difficult comments made to you. Do you think the person who spoke those words was aware of the impact? Now consider those whom your words may have impacted. Have any of these situations been resolved? If so, how?*

2. *In contrast, healed people heal people. Have you found yourself as the giver or receiver of forgiveness/reconciliation? What role did listening play in this?*

3. *Do you tend to say, "I am fine," even if you aren't? Where was this habit "caught" or "taught"? What hurdles keep you from responding truthfully?*

4. *What wounds have you left unattended? What are practical ways to nurse these wounds back to health? In this chapter, "Ellen" puts a sock on her wound and ignores it; in what ways may ignoring your wound make it worse?*

5. *Pastor Katie comments, "If women are the exception, low numbers are inevitable." Do the resources you learn through and the ministry leaders you learn from reveal women in leadership to be exceptions or the norm?*

6. *What practical step could you take this week to advocate for collaboration in these spaces?*

This Week

Write an encouragement note to a pastor or leader in or outside of your denomination. Take ten minutes to pray through a Psalm; ask the Holy Spirit to show you any area you're not "fine."

CHAPTER THREE

Missing Out: Hurdles to Discerning Kingdom-Full Vocation

I commend to you our sister Phoebe, a deacon of the church in Cenchreae. I ask you to receive her in the Lord in a way worthy of his people and to give her any help she may need from you, for she has been the benefactor of many people, including me. Greet Priscilla and Aquila, my co-workers in Christ Jesus. They risked their lives for me. Not only I but all the churches of the Gentiles are grateful to them. Greet also the church that meets at their house. Greet my dear friend Epenetus, who was the first convert to Christ in the province of Asia. Greet Mary, who worked very hard for you. Greet Andronicus and Junia, my fellow Jews who have been in prison with me. They are outstanding among the apostles, and they were in Christ before I was
(Rom. 16:1-7).

When I sensed the Holy Spirit calling me to minister as a lead pastor, I was willing to obey and follow God—but it took a leap of faith because I had a problem. Unlike the Apostle Paul, in my denomination, I had never personally known a deacon, house church co-pastor, or apostle who was a woman. I couldn't imagine how it would look. When you study to be a nurse, you start to learn many essential skills by watching an experienced healthcare worker perform them first. Then, you practice. Then, you make adjustments. No patient wants a nursing student who's never even seen an IV inserted trying to insert an IV into you!

Hurdle: Finding a Vocational Mentor

From my experience in other ministerial roles, I knew being a lead pastor would bring challenges specifically related to being a woman. I wanted to be obedient to every next step God was opening. But it felt like trying to insert an IV without ever having seen it done before.

At the same time, as deeply as I felt the need for a model of a lead pastor who was a woman, I discovered I also simply felt the need for *any* model of a lead pastor. Every area of ministry is beautiful; God equips people from all different kinds of backgrounds for a unique purpose in the body of Christ. We need youth specialists and outreach coordinators, lead pastors and hospital chaplains, translators and teachers, co-vocational ministers and administrative pastors, and many more roles.

After I entered a lead pastor role, I needed to fulfill a supervised ministry requirement by finding a professional mentor. Instead of being paired with another lead pastor, I was paired with a (wonderful) counseling pastor, solely because she was a woman. She was fantastic; she just didn't have experience as a lead pastor of a church, which was relevant to the purpose of the mentor partnering initiative. When I asked respectfully about getting a mentor with lead pastor experience given the direction my vocation was unfolding, the response was, "well, you'll understand a woman better. You can talk about anything." But what I needed was to be equipped in my role as a lead pastor.

I also needed someone internal to assess and critique my ministerial work. Again, I was encouraged to find a woman for that requirement as well. When I responded that there were no women in a position of leadership to provide that, it was suggested I find a female layperson to provide what is usually professional-level ministerial assessment and critique.

I love my church family; my dismay wasn't from a lack of trust in my church members. It was because the purpose of critique and assessment from seasoned pastors was to sharpen me as a minister of the Gospel with feedback from brothers or sisters with pastoral experience. Most church members haven't preached sermons or officiated funerals. But the conclusion was that any woman *without* pastoral experience would still be more suitable to assess me than any man *with* that experience.

Many resources on discerning calling or vocation are written with male readers in mind; few resources address the challenge of discerning vocation, giftedness, and voice in a system that has forgotten how to picture you in certain roles or how to champion God's calling on your life.

These kinds of growing pains are a sign that vital parts of the body of Christ are out of balance; or in medical terminology, they are signs of "failure to thrive." Despite a strong historical background of ordaining women for pastoral ministry, there are atrophied areas in Wesleyan/holiness denominations, muscles grown weak after long decades unused. This atrophy shows up in areas ranging from "pastors and wives" language, to uncertainty about pairing lead pastors who are women with lead pastor mentors, to navigating how work is perceived or valued. These dynamics become powerful hurdles to discernment.

Since the budget could accommodate a full-time position, he told her he needed to hire a male pastor because the job would require working closely together, which wouldn't be safe or professional if she continued. For several years, she'd already spent many hours working with him. After contributing to the church's health and growth, when the congregation was subsequently able to afford a full-time assistant pastor, she lost her job.

If anyone starting to discern a call is perceived as a novelty, hassle, liability, or source of minimally compensated volunteer work, there's room for the enemy to whisper doubt as we try to discern the Holy Spirit's guidance. A "closed door" isn't always a sign God is saying "no." Sometimes, a human is saying "no."

Hurdle: Volunteer or Colleague

One day my phone rang; it was a licensed pastor I knew professionally. For several years, she'd received a small stipend for her work as a part-time assistant pastor of a church. Now, the congregation had funds to compensate a full-time staff member in the role. She was excited that after several sacrificial years, she'd now receive a regular salary for her time and work. But after learning of the budget update, she met with the lead pastor, who informed her she would no longer be in that position. Since the budget could accommodate a full-time position, he told her he needed to hire a male pastor because the job would require working closely together, which wouldn't be safe or professional if she continued. For several years, she'd already spent many hours working with him. After contributing to the church's health and growth, when the congregation was subsequently able to afford a full-time assistant pastor, she lost her job.

She wrestled over the phone: "so the church will use me when I'm working for a stipend no one else will work for, but when they have other options, the woman has to go?" We sat over the phone in disheartened disbelief. I wondered if the ministerial journey was even possible for us. As I've coached pastors across multiple denominations, I've come to know these stories aren't unusual.

Considering situations like this, how should we hear it when preachers proclaim that if God has called you, there will be a place for you? Our world is big, and the need is great; so, while I believe with all my heart that if God calls you, God has a place for you, there's some nuance: there may not always be a place where you expect to find it or in your regional or preferred denominational context.

"I have spent so much of my time and energy fighting just to answer God's call on my life. To be denied the work of the Holy Spirit within you is a big deal." – Woman with over ten years of ministerial experience

---

Saying "yes" to God's call will always bring daunting, seemingly impossible challenges for men and women alike. But when God calls women to prepare for lead pastor roles, staff positions are a common option to gain ministerial experience before stepping into ministry as lead pastors. If lead pastors who are men decide the terms of *whether or not* men and women can work together in kingdom ministry, instead of *exploring together how we can partner in kingdom fullness in healthy ways*[1], then women will continue to encounter hurdles when searching for church roles that provide field experience in ministry. It can be hard to discern through the static, if formal roles—those that are compensated and help develop a résumé of ministerial experience—are casually, informally, but consistently reserved for pastors who are men.

And yet: when the Holy Spirit calls you and anoints you, you will find ways to minister, formally or informally, full-time or part-time. Women in the Wesleyan/holiness tradition come from a long line of sisters who preached in corn fields, worked in bi-vocational roles, revitalized rural dying churches, and sometimes were paid in fresh summer vegetables. Each of us must choose to follow wherever God leads. In our revivalistic denominations, our brothers also come from a long line of pastors who served sacrificially and often depended on God for supernatural provision.

A healthy posture toward clergy compensation in general is described in a 2022 Clergy Compensation Report from a Wesleyan/holiness denomination:

> There are some who might suggest that it is less than spiritual to draw attention to compensation, thinking that clergy should just trust God to care for them. Indeed, clergy enter Christian ministry due to a sense of calling from God, not because they think it is a lucrative career choice. However, scripture is clear that pastors should be fairly compensated for their work (1 Cor. 9:9-14; 1 Tim. 5:17-18) and it has been demonstrated that financial well-being is related to all other aspects of well-being. If clergy are not adequately compensated, it can affect other dimensions of their wellbeing such as physical and emotional health. It can also cause stress in family relationships and in the workplace. Collectively, these negative factors can result in diminished ministry effectiveness. [2]

If this is true for my brothers in pastoral leadership, it's true for my sisters as well. That same report specifies that in that setting, full-time pastors who are men have significantly higher compensation than full-time pastors who are women.[3] It is not sinful to say that that shouldn't be the case, and saying it doesn't diminish the value of the time and effort given to thousands of congregations by volunteers and pastors' spouses. That report illuminates something else: for that denomination, full-time pastors who are white are paid significantly more by congregations than full-time pastors of color. This grieves the Holy Spirit, so it should grieve us.

The enemy of our souls doesn't need to make us go down in flames in a big scandal—just to discourage us from thinking that pursuing pastoral ministry isn't a viable option. If our budgets communicate our values, what message is sent to my colleagues about the value of their labor that builds up the local body? Paul's words about Phoebe challenge us: "I ask you to receive her in the Lord in a way worthy of his people and to give her any help she may need from you, for she has been the benefactor of many people, including me" (Rom. 16:2).

Hurdle: Who We Expect to Find

Other experiences can also make room for the enemy to whisper doubt or make us feel invisible when we're trying to discern God's calling. Years into pastoral ministry, a leader who'd invested in my husband and me asked a question in surprise one day after attending a breakout session I was teaching.

"Little Katie Lance, *where* have *you* been?"

I was taken off guard. At first, I was relieved; this leader really saw me. He didn't just see me as tagging along with my husband Randy, part of a co-pastoring couple: he saw the gifting and power of the Holy Spirit in and through me.

Over time, it was repeated and felt less like a compliment. And here's one of the hard things about discerning interactions: it can be challenging when your guard is down. This wasn't on the scale of a person famous for sexist attitudes telling me to sit down, shut up, or go home. This was a valued leader who communicated in a tone of surprise, calling me "little Katie."

In situations like that, some wise, Spirit-filled mentors, coaches, counselors, or accountability partners can help you discern interactions you shouldn't take personally. I sought out some trusted insight, but I dreaded a challenging conversation or the possibility of being misunderstood. Eventually, after hours of prayer and a great deal of trust extended both ways, I had a safe, honest conversation with the leader. I mentioned the comment and answered truthfully.

"I've been here the whole time; *you just didn't see me.* You weren't looking for Katie's, you were looking for Randy's."

While I'd been desperate to be developed and equipped as a leader, my husband Randy and I were active in different areas of ministry. Randy is a wonderful man of integrity and strong leadership; I deeply respect him. He's my biggest cheerleader. Both of us participated in training environments together. Multiplication-minded leaders saw Randy's gifts and recommended next-step opportunities. During that time, I'd gleaned from what was invested in Randy. But it took time for leaders to see and champion God's calling on me as an individual, distinct from co-ministry with my husband. Gradually, over a period of years, there was a shift in how others perceived my gifts—and in how I perceived my calling.

If we equip leaders while overlooking women, what is the body of Christ missing out on? When the body of Christ shows signs of dysfunction, what can we learn from systems in the body that overlap, working together or impairing each other? When we lack called, anointed, equipped women in all levels of leadership, it doesn't just affect women who are earnestly discerning their calling and looking for role models; it also affects men and whether they instinctively picture women in all roles—including as mentors *to them*.

Multiple denominations are grappling with a shortage of pastors; pulpits standing empty as my brothers struggle on the edge of burnout. But it doesn't have to be this way. God has given us everything we need to "go and make disciples."

When significant energy is spent navigating hurdles or advocating for a seat at the leadership training table, vocational discernment becomes especially difficult. I didn't want to be "at the table" just so my voice could be heard. I just wanted to be obedient to God's calling, and I grieved that the body of Christ made it harder to say yes to God, not easier.

A Deficiency in the Body: "I've Been Missing Out"

Since I began coaching other leaders in ministry, I have lost count of the times I've been called a "unicorn" (as rare as a mythical creature). "I've heard of you, I knew lead pastors who are women were out there, but I've never actually known one." This usually comes from emerging leaders struggling to discern their calling without having seen a woman in that role. How can women picture where God is leading us, how can we dream openly, if we don't see examples in action?

Sometimes women wait decades to see what it looks like for a woman to preach the Word of God and provide spiritual leadership. When my husband and I accepted the call to co-pastor a rural church revitalization re-plant, not all the remaining legacy members were happy. As my husband and I continued ministry as co-pastors, gradually it became clear our gifting and workloads didn't match our titles. We shifted our titles to reflect our work and gifting; I became solo lead pastor while Randy worked as executive pastor.

One of our regulars caught my attention; she was a transplant from the local Baptists who joined before we arrived. God's gifting was evident in her; she was a teacher and writer of profound impact. I encouraged her to share a brief holiday reflection during worship. The Holy Spirit's anointing of her teaching was clear and powerful. Later, I invited her to "share" something…a bit longer…during Sunday worship. What she "shared" from the pulpit one Sunday morning was one of the most powerful sermons our church ever received.

Later that week, I sat on her porch swing as she wept. "I've been missing out on the fullness of what God designed me to do," she said. She was deeply grieving the unknown, wondering what God could have done throughout her life.

She's in her seventies.

I cried with her.

Meanwhile, her husband shared a different insight; he'd been profoundly moved by his wife's message that day. "I could never have received that message from God through my wife if you hadn't come here first—my heart wouldn't have been available to hear it through her."

What a regular church member shared from the pulpit one Sunday morning was one of the most powerful sermons our church ever received. Later, I sat on her porch swing as she wept. "I've been missing out on the fullness of what God designed me to do."

Church, what are we missing out on?
Who are we missing?

The witness of this couple illustrates the kingdom fullness deficiency in the body of Christ. Any healthy body requires essential nutrients and minerals like calcium, iron, vitamin C, and magnesium in balance. Without these, deficiency leads to illness, disease, and death. We can learn something important from the relationship between vitamin D and calcium.

Vitamin D is essential for healthy bone structure and muscle function; lack of vitamin D will disrupt your nervous system, musculoskeletal system, and immune system. Calcium is also essential for your body to function at full capacity: and calcium and vitamin D work together. Vitamin D and calcium can only be absorbed and used by the body once they bond together. When one is present in the body without the other, it floats free in the blood system, unabsorbed and ineffective. If your body doesn't get enough vitamin D, it starts leaching calcium from the bones, causing bone health to break down faster than it can be restored—one deficiency causing a cascade of dysfunction.

In the body of Christ, every denomination in which I mentor and coach is operating at half-capacity. When women are missing from pulpits and district and denominational leadership, there isn't just a deficiency. God designed the body of Christ to flourish in kingdom fullness, and the Church faces a cascade of dysfunction when women and men aren't partnering together. However, smoothing the path for vocational discernment will catalyze leaders. God is calling us to co-labor together in the name of Jesus Christ. We are created to work together, empowering each other's effectiveness, just like calcium and vitamin D are effective when both are active together.

What does it look like when we empower each other's effectiveness? "Greet Andronicus and Junia, my fellow Jews who have been in prison with me. They are outstanding among the apostles, and they were in Christ before I was" (Rom. 16:7). Before Paul's conversion, he hunted down early Christians, arresting and imprisoning men and women alike. By the close of his letter to the Romans, he mentions a brother and sister in Christ: Jewish Christians "who have been in prison with me." These two, he calls "outstanding among the apostles."[4]

What are we missing out on, if we settle for operating at half-capacity? When we're so accustomed to deficiency, we mistake it for health? Paul sent his greetings to Junia, describing her in a way that demonstrated how pivotal she was. His description makes clear that the body was stronger with her.

How is the body now? When a patient "codes" in crisis, alarms sound, and teams run–whose responsibility is it to sound the alarm? If a patient collapses, should a nurse wait until a more convenient moment to sound the alarm? For everyone, there's a cost to obeying the Holy Spirit and answering God's call to ministry. For some, there's a cost to naming substantive hurdles to vocational discernment. But if we don't call a "code," our brothers who want to champion God's call on their sisters won't know how best to come alongside us. Sometimes, naming hurdles leads to losing already-scarce ministry opportunities and professional partnerships, or being dismissed as overreactive, oversensitive, or hard to work with.

The point of naming hurdles isn't to focus on problems. We name hurdles because we see God's grace at work in each other, and we want each other to flourish as God intended and designed.

Many women who share their experiences are in vulnerable positions. As a lead pastor, I'm in a more stable position than if I were on staff, risking negative feedback from a senior leader. I have an incredibly supportive spouse; my husband has a pastoral position but also works independently outside the church, and our household is not solely reliant on ministerial income. I have a strong support system of mentors and coaches in and beyond my denomination. And the Holy Spirit convicts me when I see the ways God wants to unleash his kingdom force next to hurdles that make it harder to discern and follow God's calling.

Living into kingdom fullness means partnering together in ministry so that sisters and brothers in the body of Christ can help each other hear, identify, and celebrate God's calling on their lives. The kingdom of God is not a zero-sum game. Like Paul, I don't have to choose between celebrating God's grace that calls my brothers to pastoral ministry and celebrating God's grace that calls my sisters into pastoral ministry. I get to celebrate both! I thank God that in our lost, hurting world, the Holy Spirit is raising up brothers and sisters together to share the good news of Jesus Christ.

Living in kingdom fullness means naming the gifting God places in men and women alike and envisioning how their leadership might serve God's kingdom. The point of naming hurdles isn't to focus on problems; we name hurdles because we see God's grace at work in each other and we want each other to flourish as God intended and designed.

One time when my son had his vision tested, the eye doctor decided it was time for glasses. The first time those glasses slid onto his face, he looked around with wonder. "Mom! Look at the leaves on the trees! Those are faces on those signs!" Until that moment, he hadn't realized what he'd been missing.

Come, Holy Spirit. Show us where we are missing out. Give us Your vision to celebrate the fullness of the body of Christ.

Chapter Three Reflection & Discussion Questions

By Rev. Dr. Andrea Summers, Campus Pastor/Dean of Spiritual Formation for Indiana Wesleyan University

I've been mistaken for the administrative assistant or the janitorial staff more times than I can count (even while sitting in my corner office, at my desk, working at my computer!).

I've been the conference speaker who was uninvited when they found out I'm ordained.

I've been left stranded at a conference center because the male colleague who asked me to stay behind at the end of a meeting could not bend his Billy Graham rule to give me a ride back to the office.

I've had things said anonymously on social media about my body or conjectures made about my sex life that were wildly inappropriate and invasive.

These moments weren't fun, but much more difficult to navigate have been the countless and compounding subtle hurdles that sometimes leave me second-guessing my perception:

- *Whenever a conversation partner makes eye contact with my husband and looks right past me.*

- *The times a couple I've deeply invested in chooses a man they barely know to perform their wedding vows.*

- *Sensing I've disappointed people when they realize my gifts are less nurturing and more galvanizing.*

If I'm being honest, I rarely talk about these experiences and hesitate to put them in writing, because I don't want to be perceived as complaining or "too sensitive." But there is no getting around the fact that it's jarring and surreal to bump into barriers while others around you tell you barriers don't exist.

Everyone faces challenges in ministry, but some of the challenges women encounter are unique. It is a difficult thing to address "the elephant in the room" when those who are in the best position to do something about the elephant do not see it or are unaware of the ways it is impacting their choices.

This is why it is so important for both women and men to understand the unique hurdles that women face. Yes, there is the theological hurdle—the reality that over half of Christians already have a theological orientation that opposes women in positions of spiritual authority. But there are also barriers that Katie unpacked for us relating to seasons of life, relational distancing, and unspoken perceptions and expectations. When we name these hurdles, they don't disappear, but naming them makes it possible for men and women to lead through them together.

I say men and women because these hurdles are not just holding women back from becoming all God has called us to be. The profound loss here is that the image of the kingdom of God revealed to the world is warped and incomplete. The harvest is plentiful and the workers are few, but even the workers we have are fatigued and facing burnout.

In God's kingdom, the outpouring of the Holy Spirit raises up our sons and our daughters. A true kingdom vision reflects the possibility of partnering with God and each other in ways that honor Genesis 1-2. It is possible to co-labor shoulder to shoulder for the sake of the Gospel as Paul did with the women of Romans 16. It is possible to begin practicing now the restoration of all things in a way that leans toward Revelation's vision for eternity.

Discussion Questions

1. *Can you remember a time when you experienced (or witnessed someone else experience) a hurdle to their growth, gifts, or calling? How did God show up in that instance?*

2. *One woman's spiritual gifts showed up for decades through her writing and teaching; however, she was over seventy before she preached her first sermon. Have you ever heard a woman give a message from the pulpit? Think about people in your life who have discovered gifts or calling at different stages of life. What does this say about God's character, who he calls, and how he calls them?*

3. *Katie's son didn't know what he was missing until he slid glasses onto his face for the first time. Ask God to give you vision for the church that includes kingdom fullness. What do you see? Describe it out loud into your phone's voice memo app or journal about it now.*

This Week

For our brothers–church members, pastors' husbands, bi-vocational ministers, part or full-time pastors, volunteers: *This month, pray, then reach out to one pastor who's a woman and ask for just one thing you can do to champion God's call on her life. If she's not in your district or denomination anymore, try to find out where she is; pray, and if you feel led, reach out and see if it's okay to ask why she's not in a particular region or denomination anymore.*

For our sisters–pastors' wives, bi-vocational ministers, volunteers, and part or full-time pastors: *This month, track the number of hours you spend on kingdom work, not because you're "counting the cost," but so that you can be honest with yourself about your time,* resources, and so that you value your contribution and work. For my sisters looking for formal ministerial positions, review ways to shape and include volunteer or stipend work as experience on résumés.

For everyone, from pews to pulpit: Track where your time goes in kingdom work for a month or two to help you name responsibilities, skills, and accomplishments that you're sometimes too busy to describe, recall, or capture. Notice where your time goes, which parts you love, and which parts are stressors. This will help you discern your gifting, passions, strengths, and what kind of season your soul may need next.

CHAPTER FOUR

Catalyzing Leaders:
Cultivating Kingdom Fullness

*"Sanctify them in the truth; your word is truth. As you,
Father, are in me and I am in you, may they also be in us,
so that the world may believe that you have sent me.
The glory that you have given me I have given them, so that
they may be one, as we are one, I in them and you in me,
that they may become completely one, so that the world
may know that you have sent me and have loved them even
as you have loved me"* (John 17:17, 21b-23).

*"It makes me sick when I see a guy just stare at a loose ball
and watch it go out of bounds." -NBA Hall of Famer,
All-Star, and MVP Larry Bird*

Larry Bird loved to play the game of basketball, he loved to play it well, and he loved to win. As good as he was, he knew something simple: it's a team sport. It drove him crazy to see teammates fail to take advantage of low-hanging fruit, like a loose ball up for grabs. After all, for your team to score, you need the ball!

Seeing a moment and seizing it is important in medicine, too. When a patient who receives inconsistent care is sitting in front of you, that's the moment to check their prescription refills, connect them with resources, and engage in patient education. There are other times in medicine when it's vital to seize the moment: when a patient is critical, healthcare workers must realize what's happening and apply their experience and knowledge to intervene *now*.

Jesus said, "Don't you have a saying, 'It's still four months until harvest'? I tell you, open your eyes and look at the fields! They are ripe for harvest. Even now the one who reaps draws a wage and harvests a crop for eternal life, so that the sower and the reaper may be glad together" (John 4:35-36). Jesus said this to his disciples while their minds were on their lunches, oblivious to what was happening in the bigger picture. They had stopped to get something to eat in a Samaritan town and brought Jesus his food, but Jesus wasn't thinking about lunch anymore—the Samaritan woman had just forgotten her water jar at the well, running off into town to tell everyone who she'd just met. Jesus and his disciples were about to spend a couple of days in this Samaritan village: the Messiah, bringing the good news to Samaritans.

Jesus and Larry Bird are both shouting, "There's a loose ball! Don't just stand there, go get it! The Samaritans are ready to believe; stop thinking about lunch, there's been a change of plans, something's stirring in this town—don't you see the moment? Don't you see? Everything's ripe for the harvest!"

Once we're in the habit of naming and creatively dismantling hurdles to kingdom fullness, then the fun part begins: catalyzing leaders for the great commission.

Jesus asked us to be ready, warmed up, and focused so that we can live out the great commission in community together. God is calling us to love others like Jesus loved, to make disciple-makers, to celebrate the life of the body of Christ. Once we're in the habit of naming and creatively dismantling hurdles to kingdom fullness, then the fun part begins: catalyzing leaders for the great commission.

When every teammate is expectant and equipped with their "eye on the ball," the Holy Spirit can prompt our initiative, forming in us the readiness to see and seize critical moments. When we're sensitive to the Spirit, the body of Christ can function like a healthy, strong, versatile team that is enlivened by the Spirit of God. Cultivating kingdom fullness creates space for God to call, equip, and anoint people who will be able to reach people that you or I never could. As Paul wrote, "I planted the seed, Apollos watered it, but God has been making it grow" (I Cor. 3:6).

God has given us everything we need to live out the great commission. It just takes humility to be comfortable with our limitations: even Larry Bird couldn't win if he tried to play against another team by himself. The Holy Spirit is still providing what God said we needed in the very beginning: it's not good for a human to be alone. God is still giving us company, fellowship, teammates, sisters and brothers, and coworkers in the Gospel. If we hustle to claim loose basketballs, proactively committing to raising up both men and women in leadership, then some of our challenges—empty pulpits, burnt-out pastors, the call to multiply—will take care of themselves. "Open your eyes and look at the fields! They are ripe for harvest."

God is calling us to wake up to this moment; this moment is not an idealized moment or a hypothetical moment. The Holy Spirit is asking us to be ready to respond to the moment we have. What are some ways we can do that? Let's look at:

- How to orient ourselves to the opportunity of this unique moment
- Ways we can catalyze leaders for the great commission
- How to cultivate a culture of kingdom fullness

You Are Here: Getting Our Bearings

When Jesus and his disciples traveled through Samaria and stopped at Jacob's well, they didn't have a rest area with a large map displaying a big red arrow and the words, "you are here." There weren't billboards. Jewish people usually avoided Samaria; they deliberately didn't travel through it. For Jesus' disciples, this territory wasn't as familiar as their home turf.

That sense of disorientation or the instinct to hurry through and get back to solid footing—does that sound familiar? Does any of that ring true with so much rapid technological and post-pandemic global change? We've had a lot to process.

If we want our congregations to be ready and equipped to chase after a "loose basketball" (to see a moment ripe for harvest) then let's quickly get our bearings and name a few of the challenges of this moment. Some of these are especially true in North America, and some are relevant wherever you are in the world.

- Many American pastors and church leaders were part of the large Baby Boom generation; over the past ten years, they began retiring. The generations coming up behind them are simply smaller with fewer people.
- Most people know someone who died of COVID-19 or whose ability to work has been affected by "long" COVID. Across

denominations, there are pastors, long-serving lay leaders, and church members we lost. Many people are still grieving.

- Some American pastors and church leaders were part of the "great resignation" after 2020, as workers across professions reevaluated their schedules, vocations, and priorities.

- Budgets and leadership have had to adjust as uneven economic and workforce recovery have an ongoing impact on our churches.

- In short, there are congregations with pulpits standing empty. There are congregations still processing losses, and congregations with challenging budgetary realities.

In pews and pulpits, there's a lot of grief, burnout, and a sense of urgency, as well; where do we go from here? Maybe you resonate with the disciples on the road to Emmaus, who were "downcast" - "but we had hoped…" (Luke 24:21).

You arrived at a new church in 2019, energized and ready, and now you're exhausted: "we had hoped."

You started your ordination process, but progress slowed when you were laid off and had to find three part-time jobs to try to make up the difference: "we had hoped."

You'd planned on retiring in 2020, but when a crisis occurred, you knew retiring would add uncertainty and strain, so you kept going. Now, instead of concluding full-time ministry on a high note, it's hard not to look out and tally the losses: "we had hoped."

You started ministry as a second-career pastor, but your spouse got sick and passed away, and it's been hard to focus ever since: "we had hoped."

Those downcast disciples walking to Emmaus didn't walk alone.

Something flared to life as they walked and talked; "they asked each other, 'were not our hearts burning within us while he talked with us on the road and opened the Scriptures to us?'" (Luke 24:32; some scholars like N.T. Wright suggest the likelihood that these two disciples of Jesus were a married couple on the way back to their house[1]).

On their way home, the disciples had been bewildered and disoriented. Now, they couldn't deny their hearts burning. Hope reignited as they walked in Jesus' presence, even before they recognized him.

Jesus shows up for the disoriented and the discouraged.

Not that long after that walk, the church was birthed on Pentecost in the upper room where women and men were gathered praying.

The church was born in the middle of people who were still grieving what Judas had done; it was born in the middle of people who had grieved their shortcomings, like Simon Peter; it was born in the middle of people who were terrified they might be next in line for arrest.

The church was born through the Holy Spirit, in the middle of people who had been through profound disorientation, for people who needed the power of Christ to reorient their lives to God's kingdom. If we want to talk about living through rapid change, read through Luke and Acts. The disciples and apostles were constantly readjusting—even after the resurrection; even after Pentecost, after being filled with the Holy Spirit.

Disorientation is where we have been, but it is not who we are.

The Holy Spirit unleashes who we are when we allow God to reorient us toward Christ through life as his body. Our identity is in Christ, and kingdom fullness is the overflow of that reality.

This means that if circumstances, change, loss, and upheaval couldn't define the early believers anointed with the power of God, they aren't what define the body of Christ today. They can be powerful. They're a very real part of our story. They shouldn't be denied or ignored. But they are not the *end* of the story. This is how we can carry grief, sadness, and frustration in one hand while we carry strangely burning hearts in the other.

Jesus was so patient with those early disciples walking the road to Emmaus; he walked them through their grief and walked them through the scriptures. Then he gave them space, waiting for their invitation. And when their disorientation had been placed in his presence and held in the preciousness of God's Word, when their hearts strangely flickered to life and they invited him to stay, then and only then Jesus allowed them to recognize who was sitting at their table.

God doesn't rush us.

Jesus walks next to us.

And we don't talk about catalyzing leaders so we can use them as a means to an end, as a way of meeting a pragmatic need; we also care for their souls as people whose disorientation is worth our time as we walk along the road.

It's only in this context that we can look around, free to ask: in this unique moment, what opportunity might there be? For the disciples in Emmaus, thunderstruck at the unique moment that unfolded, they immediately took the opportunity to head straight back to Jerusalem to tell the other disciples they'd just seen Jesus.

In our unique moment, what opportunities might be present? Is there a moment to seize, leaning into God's provision of kingdom fullness as we live the great commission? Is there a moment that's been lost, that you need to let go of so you can receive this one with open hands? Are you ready to invite Christ into this moment that you have?

Like the disciples walking to Emmaus, are you familiar with holding disorientation in one hand, and burning hearts in the other? What is the Holy Spirit asking you to see in this moment and about this moment? What is God asking you to believe, in this moment and about this moment? What does God's heart of love want to say to you today?

I am praying that today you hear the depth and fullness of God's love. I am praying God's grace heals the frustration of lost moments and makes things new. I am praying the Holy Spirit brings the love of Jesus so close that your heart burns within you at the hope springing up.

There are no best practices, habits, organizational changes, podcasts, or seminars that can replace the power of the Holy Spirit stirring up our awareness of Jesus' presence.

That means that when we explore ways to catalyze leaders, we recognize that these methods are secondary tools used in response to the work of God in us and the presence of Christ in our midst.

Ways to Catalyze Leaders for the Great Commission

When I'm coaching, I pray. It's the Holy Spirit who calls people and works in their hearts, not me. When I'm interacting with people, I'm also trying to listen to the Holy Spirit, trusting God to use my experiences and gifts and to grow my discernment. I'm not the only one praying; I have people pouring into my life, praying for me. If we truly believe God's promises, we can't ignore the power of prayer.

Above any other priority, if you want to catalyze leaders for a culture of kingdom fullness, start with prayer. It doesn't get fancier or easier than that. As Dr. Jo Anne Lyon (General Superintendent

Emerita of The Wesleyan Church) has reminded me, "Pray in a clear, unambiguous direction."

These are some of the things I pray for:

- I ask God to begin providing the relationships that will nurture kingdom fullness. That's a prayer that God will always answer. "This is the confidence we have in approaching God: that if we ask anything according to his will, he hears us" (I John 5:14).

- I pray for teams I work with, that they catch God's vision for kingdom fullness in the body of Christ and grow through solid discipleship and multiplication.

- I pray for God's will to be done on earth, as it is in heaven. I know the beauty of God's vision for a healthy, versatile body of Christ, and I ask that it is God's will for this to be done here and now.

In this context of prayer—as I pray and as others pray over me—there are ways I can catalyze leaders God is calling and equipping for kingdom fullness. When I longed to be developed as a leader, I sought out ways to grow as a leader. Now when I encounter others, my habit is to see the flame of their gifting, "pour gasoline on it," and give people the opportunity and freedom to grow. These are some ways to catalyze leaders for the great commission:

- Bring people with you wherever you go. If I'm going to a conference, a hospital bedside, or a district meeting, I'm taking an emerging leader with me.

- Empower leaders by making space for established leaders to "rub shoulders" with emerging leaders.

- Identify ways to expand the leadership pipeline by knowing and empowering women currently in ministry.

- Identify ways to empower men to follow God's call to equip the body for thriving in kingdom fullness.

As I continue to grow and develop as a leader, I practice habits like these:

- If I sense God leading me into something new, I find people to ask questions about it. Then, I ask each of them for three more people I can ask questions.
- Listening to the Holy Spirit's guidance and prompting, I pursue cross-denominational leadership spaces. Early on as I pursued development as a leader, I went to gatherings where I didn't need an invitation, putting myself "on the radar" and initiating presence.
- I seek out mentors (men and women) who will coach and teach me.

These are a few practical ways to catalyze women and men into pastoral and church leadership as we look for ways to respond to this moment with kingdom fullness.

How to Cultivate a Culture of Kingdom Fullness

Jesus' prayer for us in John 17 is a beautiful picture of the nature of kingdom fullness. "As you, Father, are in me and I am in you, may they also be in us, so that the world may believe that you have sent me. The glory that you have given me I have given them, so that they may be one, as we are one, I in them and you in me, that they may become completely one, so that the world may know that you have sent me and have loved them even as you have loved me" (John 17:21b-23).

When we are completely one in Christ, God in Christ, and Christ in us, what is the natural overflow?

"So that the world may know that you have sent me and have loved them."

This is what happens when we receive Christ in our midst and live kingdom fullness in response. God has tasked us with stewarding this moment well and gave us the Holy Spirit so we have the power and discernment to do so.

So first, what does it look like if a church culture is missing out on kingdom fullness? You know you're missing kingdom fullness if:

- Talk and energy revolve around how to get a moment in church life back instead of how the Spirit is inviting us to receive and respond to this unique moment (Luke 24:19-21a).

- Energy is spent on multiplication or "doing for God" before attending to discipleship and abiding with God (John 15:5).

- There are more legacy leaders than emerging leaders (Matt. 20:20-27).

- Membership and leadership do not reflect the demographics of the region where you live, worship, and carry out ministry (Acts 2:5-11).

- Energy is spent maintaining current comfort rather than responding to uncertain opportunities (John 4:27-33).

- Established leaders and volunteers are burned out but don't have the tools, energy, desire, or opportunity to recruit others or pass on their roles and responsibilities to emerging leaders (Exodus 18:13-23).

- The work of the church is carried out "to the letter of the law" but without the fruits or gifts of the Spirit (Mark 10:17-22).

When the body of Christ shows symptoms lacking kingdom fullness, we know that nothing replaces the presence and work of the Holy Spirit. There's no tool, hack, or app for that. Sometimes, God's grace appears as moments of opportunity: a chance for us to find ways to say yes to the Holy Spirit when we lay out everything on the altar and desire the work of Jesus in our hearts, churches, and communities.

Now, what might happen if we find ways to say yes to the promptings of the Holy Spirit? What could emerge if we say yes to increasing opportunities for half of the body of Christ to respond to God's call in all areas of ministry, in local churches, denominational leadership, and beyond? Could cultivating a culture of kingdom fullness create space for half of the body of Christ to say yes to God's call?

Cultivating kingdom culture always flows over into catalyzing leaders; catalyzing leaders is one way we cultivate kingdom culture. And we cultivate kingdom culture the ways Christians always have. We do it by:

- Praying; getting in step with the Holy Spirit.
- Repenting, personally and corporately, as the Holy Spirit convicts us.
- Pursuing healing, repairing, and unifying conversations through deep listening.
- Practicing alertness and discernment against the enemy's schemes to divide.
- Watching for God's activity in our denominations and the universal church.

Frequently, I coach leaders who want to develop a culture of kingdom fullness. Sometimes we discuss questions leaders can ask themselves if they want to champion a culture of kingdom fullness that catalyzes leaders who are women. Are you leading a culture of kingdom fullness that creates space for women to say yes to God, however the Holy Spirit gifts and calls them? Here are some questions to ask:

- Who are the clergywomen who lead in your congregation's ministry or preached in Sunday morning worship over the last year? Can you write down their names and the dates they preached (dates not including Mother's Day)?
- Do you have colleagues who are women who you intentionally and consistently lead and learn with and from?
- Who are the women you are raising up to say their next "yes" to God?
- Who are the women on your boards, leadership, and staff (beyond children's, women's, worship, and global mission ministries)?

Questions like these aren't meant to be a tally or checklist; they're helpful because our specific practices can indicate any gap existing between our values and our habits. How did this chapter open? "It makes me sick when I see a guy just stare at a loose ball and watch it go out of bounds." Questions like these are helpful tools because none of us wants to be the player Larry Bird is yelling at while we are absentmindedly watching a loose ball go out of bounds instead of fighting for it.

If that's true for a game, *how much more is it true* when Jesus is redirecting our attention to a moment ripe for harvest? For some reason, God allows us (you and me!) to participate in the beauty of his kingdom. God has poured out and stored up the Holy Spirit on us and in us for something much bigger than a basketball game.

Asking how we're cultivating a culture of kingdom fullness can prompt us to keep our focus on the Holy Spirit's action. God has given us everything we need to live the great commission with joy and hope. We have the Holy Spirit, who flickers life and hope into flame in our hearts when we're disoriented and downcast. We have what we need to receive and respond to this moment—not the moment we wish we had, or the moment we missed, or the moment we think others are having—but this moment.

When I pray, God fills me with hope and joy to see his kingdom fullness displayed. I don't want to miss the moment right in front of me. I want to pay attention to the ways my heart is burning within me along the road; I want to invite Christ in, God in Christ, and Christ in us so that the body of Christ can become "completely one, so that the world may know" how deeply God loves it!

Come, Holy Spirit! Mobilize us in Your power and joy so that the world may know how deep Your love is.

Chapter Four Reflection & Discussion Questions

By Rev. Dr. Ken Schenck, Provost, CampusEdu; Biblical Scholar

As I remarked after first encountering this book, the thing about blind spots is that you don't see them. It's hard to be fully effective with one eye closed.

Discussion Questions

1. *As you look around you in your church setting, where is the ball not being picked up? Who is there in your midst who could be in the game but is not on the court?*

2. *What opportunities has God put right in front of us that we are missing because we don't have our "eye on the ball"?*

3. *You wouldn't intentionally play a game with two or three players missing from the field. Who are we not seeing right now who needs to be in the game?*

This Week

Identify one person in your context who is not in the game but should be. Especially focus on individuals who might be overlooked or "unseen" because we're not looking in their direction. Strategize to increasingly include them in the mission of the church over the next few months in some specific way that the Holy Spirit leads.

CHAPTER FIVE

Why The Wesleyan/Holiness Movement Settled for Less than Kingdom Fullness

"Nothing but jealousy, prejudice and bigotry and a stingy love for bossing in men have prevented women's public recognition by the church. No church that is acquainted with the Holy Ghost will object to the public ministry of women." – Seth C. Rees (1854-1933), a preacher known as the "earthquaker"[1] and founder of The Pilgrim Holiness Church, a parent denomination of The Wesleyan Church.

You know, I don't expect anyone to agree with everything in this book—but I get the sense that any time my tone may seem blunt, it's nothing compared to our spiritual grandfather Seth Rees!

Every day in the life of the church that extends around the globe, we practice default habits. For better or worse, my habits reveal my values. No Christian is completely, perfectly consistent; we all fall short of the glory of God. Each of us has a deep capacity for self-deception. But if you say you value your health and then never pursue the healthcare that's available to you or attempt to fill a basic prescription, I'll struggle to take your words seriously.

You may *want* to value your health—you may just not realize how easy it is to lose.

Ideally in the church, our habits don't contradict our expressed beliefs; they illustrate them. On paper, denominations like The Wesleyan Church and others affirm women in all roles of pastoral leadership. What do we do, then, if our practices fall short of our doctrine, heritage, and most importantly our scriptural witness anointed by the Holy Spirit?

At various points in Pilgrim [Holiness] history, thirty or more percent of all ministers were women. The Pilgrims also ordained deaconesses. – Dr. Lee Haines

---

There is a significant difference between going along with the idea of women leading in pastoral ministry and proactively pursuing habits that recruit, equip, and champion women in senior leadership, denominational, and lead pastor positions.

The Divide: Missing Pastors in the Twentieth Century

Many Wesleyan/Holiness denominations in the U.S. have a strong heritage of celebrating women in the pulpit. Wesleyan/Holiness leaders in the United States supported the ordination of women over 100 years ago. In the past, the parent denominations of The Wesleyan Church (The Pilgrim Holiness Church and The Wesleyan Methodist Church) along with leaders of the Free Methodist Church, the Church of the Nazarene, the Church of God, the Salvation Army, and the Christian and Missionary Alliance[2] all found a variety of ways to celebrate women responding to the call to preach. Historians from denominations like these have shared rich resources on the history of women preachers, pastors, superintendents, and evangelists in America over the past 150 years (*Celebrate Our Daughters: 150 Years of Women in Wesleyan Ministry* by Maxine L. Haines and Lee M. Haines is a great place to start). Here are just a few highlights from holiness history:

- In 1853, Wesleyan Methodist minister Rev. Luther Lee preached "A Woman's Right to Preach the Gospel," ordaining Congregationalist Miss Antoinette Brown.

- Co-founder of The Salvation Army Catherine Booth published a pamphlet in 1859 called "Female Ministry, or Woman's Right to Preach the Gospel."

- By 1870 the Salvation Army officially outlined the full participation of women at any rank and in preaching and decision-making.

- In 1891, the founder of the Free Methodist Church, B.T. Roberts, argued in support of women in pastoral leadership in *Ordaining Women*, though it took his denomination time to put his arguments into practice.[3]

- In 1894, Rev. Julia Foote was ordained a deacon in the historic Black AME Zion Church; she was the second woman in that denomination to become an ordained elder in 1899.

- Since its organization in 1908, the Church of the Nazarene has recognized the Holy Spirit's calling on women to preach and pastor.[4]

In 1968, The Pilgrim Holiness Church and The Wesleyan Methodist Church merged, forming The Wesleyan Church. By that time, both denominations already had a long history of ordaining women for pastoral ministry. According to the late Dr. Lee M. Haines, "at various points in Pilgrim history, thirty or more percent of all ministers were women. The Pilgrims also ordained deaconesses."[5]

"I felt gifted, but not called to the roles I was able to secure. I knew God called me to be a lead pastor, but there were no churches for me. After all this time, it was abundantly clear that I needed to go somewhere else." – Woman with decades of ministerial experience who changed denominations

---

But around the time of the merger, the American cultural landscape was changing, and the church leadership landscape changed with it. Wesleyan/holiness denominations had concluded the 1940s with a strong cohort of seasoned, ordained women who'd been active in pastoral leadership for decades. Yet by 1974, Donald Dayton and Lucille Sider Dayton noted the decline in a paper called "Women in the Holiness Movement" presented in a seminar at the Christian Holiness Association convention.

So where did all the ordained women go?

War, Bureaucracy, Social Status, Women's Liberation

If a significant portion of church leaders drops "off the radar" in the span of a few years, it's worth taking notice. There were multiple dynamics influencing established Wesleyan/holiness denominations and newly merged ones like The Wesleyan Church. For now, let's look at a couple of basic factors.

In 1993—thirty years before *this* book—Dr. Rebecca Laird questioned the absence of women preachers at that time in the Church of the Nazarene in the context of her own denomination's amazing heritage of ordaining women. "The influence of ordained women has decreased markedly over the years. Later generations have not renewed the church's historic legacy of women vigorously entering the ordained ministry. As a result, many people… are beginning to ask why proportionately fewer women presently serve the church as active ordained elders. I began to ask, 'Where are the women preachers now?' I looked around for role models and found few. I knew women *could* serve the church in any capacity. Yet they weren't."[6] Laird identified a couple of key dynamics that shifted her Wesleyan/holiness denomination away from its heritage:

- The gradual drift from a strong shared experience of the outpouring of the Holy Spirit in the 1800s to a top-heavy bureaucratic structure tasked with steering ordination processes and candidates.
- A backlash against the secular women's liberation movement in the 1960s and 70s, "led some to believe that redefining a Christian woman's primary place of influence as the home is the only way to maintain family strength."[7]

For these denominations, including mine, the scriptural foundation for women's ordination had been established decades (or even more than a century) before. In the case of The Wesleyan Church, both parent denominations entered the merger strengthened in part by years of fruitful ministry from their pastors who were women.

But by the 1960s, multiple dynamics were at work. As Laird identified with the Nazarenes, The Wesleyan Church also became less movement and more institution, formalizing clergy training and ordination processes. This reality overlapped with workforce pressures after World War II, when there was an explicit societal push to place returning veterans in work and women were encouraged to focus on domestic life. At the same time, Rev. Maxine and Rev. Lee Haines noted a socioeconomic shift in their carefully collected volume of biographies of women preachers and pastors in Wesleyan/holiness denominations. They explained, "the holiness churches had often been characterized as being 'on the wrong side of the tracks.' There was now a deliberate move 'across the tracks' to more 'strategic' locations."[8] This was relevant especially because, as Rev. and Rev. Haines noted,

> Often [women] received difficult appointments that men would not accept and were told at the outset that they would be replaced by a man as soon as the church could support and man and his family. Women had often single-handedly planted churches, and then brought them into one of the denominations. But by the 1950s, church planting was more structured and more centered on the role of the district or conference. The churches planted by women in the past had often been assigned male pastors soon after coming into one of the denominations. The new church-planting program was thus somewhat conditioned to the selection of male pastors. The interests of the denominations were shifting away from deprived persons and rural or small-town situations to urban and suburban settings.[9]

Essentially, women ministered in areas and contexts where no one else would go and planted churches where no one else wanted to serve. As denominations sought respectability and moved away from ministry "on the wrong side of the tracks," church planting was centralized.

> *Women ministered in areas and contexts where no one*
> *else would go and planted churches where no one else*
> *wanted to serve. As denominations sought respectability*
> *and moved away from ministry "on the wrong side of the*
> *tracks," church planting was centralized.*

In "Women in the Holiness Movement," Lucille Sider Dayton and Donald Dayton illuminated this move toward respectability and the role of social pressure: "...in each instance and at each stage of development the Holiness stance [toward the ordination of women] was generally in advance of the positions taken by other traditions. This practice continued well into the 20th century, but has declined in recent years. With the rising social status of the Holiness denominations and the consequent socialization to dominant society, this distinctive pattern has become more a memory than a living reality."[10]

The early Wesleyan/holiness movement was fostered by preachers and pastors from very humble backgrounds; a lot of its leaders were very poor. In the late 1800s and early 1900s, it was frequently the upper classes that promoted strict gender roles. The Daytons' point was that as the holiness movement became upwardly mobile, it had also become self-conscious in the face of social pressure.

Just as the Wesleyan/holiness denominations had been fitting in with societal expectations of gender roles, the 1960s and 70s erupted into an era of women's liberation and women's rights. (In the United States, it was 1974 before women were guaranteed the legal right to open a bank account without a male co-signer's signature.) If we ask which came first in the United States— women preaching, teaching, and being ordained, or the women's liberation movement of the 1960s and 70s—women preachers came first across multiple denominations by a wide margin of multiple decades or even a century. But despite a fruitful history ordaining women for pastoral leadership, multiple Wesleyan/ holiness denominations reacted strongly to some secular movements, as Dr. Laird demonstrated. In the process, they ignored their heritage in reaction to societal shifts.

Rather than responding to societal change by pursuing a sanctified, scriptural vision of anointing for leadership, some Wesleyan/ holiness leaders and denominations quietly adopted a posture that muted Seth C. Rees and other founders who lived seventy or a hundred years earlier. Despite a long-standing scriptural foundation, the impassioned arguments of holiness denominations' founders, and decades of effective pastoral ministry provided by women, a new posture emerged. If culture celebrated the women's liberation definitions of equality, then the safest position for holiness denominations was to distance themselves even from their own roots. (The Christian Holiness Association illustrated this in 1972 by issuing a poorly nuanced resolution that prompted the Daytons' responding paper in the first place.[10])

But there was ample material to help Wesleyan/holiness leaders feel justified in their reactions. Another factor at the time contributed to the disappearance of women in pastoral leadership: the overwhelming availability of resources that were not shaped by scriptural Wesleyan/holiness theology. In *Celebrate Our Daughters*, Rev. Lee and Rev. Maxine Haines note that, "both the Wesleyan Methodist and Pilgrim Holiness leaders and ministers joined the broadstream evangelical movement in the newly organized National Association of Evangelicals. This brought them into contact with leaders from other churches that held a male-dominated worldview. Many evangelicals totally opposed the ordination of women, and holiness people began to read their writings and follow them on radio and television."[12]

If you've ever seen a diagram of multiple open umbrellas stacked over each other, the largest labeled "Christ" over the next labeled "husband," and Christ and husband umbrellas both over "wife," then you've seen the theology that flooded Christian bookstores and churches in the 1960s, 70s, and 80s. Popular leaders who didn't share Wesleyan/holiness theology gained influence under Wesleyan roofs, identifying ideas like the "umbrella" hierarchy with family values.

What happens when church members or even pastors accept an interpretation of scripture that places men between women and God? Do we believe in the priesthood of all believers—that through Christ, all believers have direct access to God? The "umbrella" example shifts the priesthood of all believers to the priesthood of believing men, in which a woman's husband (or father) has an intermediary role between a woman and God. In 2003 research on equipping women for leadership in the setting of a Wesleyan church, Dr. Gaile Smith clearly described the relationship between the idea of the priesthood of all believers and women ministering in church leadership.[11]

The flood of resources supporting "complementarian" interpretations of Christian marriage was difficult to reconcile with historic Wesleyan Methodist holiness theology and practice. A complementarian model of marriage insists on fixed roles that are said to "complement" or work with each other. Complementarians believe men are the implicit and explicit heads and spiritual leaders of households. Sometimes this model extends to husbands "standing in" for God so that the best way for a woman to submit to God is to submit to the leadership of her husband in all matters, large or small. (In one book for Christian women written a few decades ago, the author gives an example of disagreeing with her husband over a lamp; her husband decided he didn't like the lamp, so, to submit to God by submitting to her husband, she returned the lamp she loved.)

At its worst, a complementarian model of Christian marriage has been used to keep women and children in dangerous situations and environments of abuse. At its best, it's been used to establish a universal marriage model in the home that makes it nearly impossible to simultaneously celebrate the Holy Spirit's anointing of women to preach the Gospel of Jesus Christ. How can we assert that husbands are the sole spiritual leaders of a household while testifying that the Holy Spirit anoints and equips women to preach to the body of Christ—not only other women, or children, but to the entire body of Christ—with authority?

An "egalitarian" model of Christian marriage harmonizes beautifully with the New Testament vision for kingdom fullness and flourishing. The egalitarian model celebrates the outpouring of the Holy Spirit with authority on all believers, men and women, sisters and brothers, husbands and wives, side by side. Decision-making, responsibility, and authority are shared according to the varying gifts, interests, strengths, and aptitudes of individuals. For believers who are married, there may be differing seasons or stages when a couple passes responsibilities back and forth depending on the demands of that time and context. This flexibility doesn't cost men some specific picture of masculinity any more than Jesus washing and drying his disciples' feet cost him his. It doesn't cost women some specific picture of femininity any more than Mary learning at Jesus' feet with his other disciples instead of cooking with her sister cost her hers.

So with dynamics like *increased institutional bureaucracy, cultural pressure, and a surge of complementarian marriage materials,* the environment across Wesleyan/holiness denominations chilled quickly for ordained women. Did our denominations officially support the ordination of women? Yes—but congregations and districts absorbing non-Wesleyan theology like the "umbrella" paradigm were hardly a welcoming, encouraging environment for women to explore a call to pastoral ministry. Missions, children's ministry, unpaid volunteer work, and church planting became the primary accepted outlets to live out what was formerly identified as a call.

Our Wesleyan/holiness zeal for a sanctified vision of scripturally reckoned leadership chilled: we lost our fervor to see anointed leaders partnering side by side. Would Seth C. Rees think we settled for what was in arm's reach, what was socially expedient, what seemed safe? If we did compromise, we compromised for less than God's lively design, promises, and power for the body of Christ.

Any time the church falls short in how sisters and brothers in Christ relate to each other, it's tempting to think the divide exists between men and women. That is where some of the visible cost lands.

Ultimately, the divide at the foundations of Wesleyan/holiness denominations wasn't between brothers and sisters in ministry. It wasn't even primarily between church and culture. *The divide was where it's always been for Christians: between what we profess and what we do.* A gap widened between our shared story of beliefs and values about women in pastoral ministry and the story our actions told.

Maybe there was also a divide between our testimony to the Holy Spirit's power shaping the kingdom of God, and our actual choices when we reacted to cultural change.

How can we pinpoint that this is the underlying divide? Because we ignored our well-documented heritage of scriptural foundations and practice. We tried to edit our DNA. We turned to theology that contradicted our history and understanding of scripture.

The Holy Spirit gives us everything we need to live kingdom-full as the healthy body of Christ. Yet Wesleyan/holiness denominations became embarrassed to champion women in leadership. We became convinced that continuing to embrace women in pastoral leadership looked like we were being led by cultural shifts.

Implicitly or explicitly, we concluded that women in our pulpits or district offices could compromise the effectiveness of our witness rather than amplify it. We shelved the testimonies and fruitful ministries of ranks of women preaching and pastoring in the 1800s and early 1900s. What scripture comes to mind? Like the Israelites so often in the Old Testament, we looked around, got overwhelmed, hesitated at God's promises and power—and forgot who, and Whose, we are.

But *unlike* the Israelites, you and I and our sisters and brothers in Christ around the globe have the convicting, empowering, illuminating presence of the Holy Spirit poured out on us. Should our reaction to societal change determine our actions? Or should the Holy Spirit breathe life into our beliefs, empowering us to bear witness to the fullness of God? In Ephesians 1, the Apostle Paul wrote,

> I keep asking that the God of our Lord Jesus Christ, the glorious Father, may give you the Spirit of wisdom and revelation, so that you may know him better. I pray that the eyes of your heart may be enlightened in order that you may know the hope to which he has called you, the

riches of his glorious inheritance in his holy people, *and his incomparably great power for us who believe. That power is the same as the mighty strength he exerted when he raised Christ from the dead and seated him at his right hand in the heavenly realms, far above all rule and authority, power and dominion, and every name that is invoked, not only in the present age but also in the one to come.* And God placed all things under his feet and appointed him to be head over everything for the church, which is his body, the fullness of him who fills everything in every way (Ephesians 1:16-23).

Brothers and sisters, what are we doing with the hope to which God has called us—what are we doing with the riches of God's glorious inheritance in his holy people? What are we doing with God's incomparably great power for us who believe?

One Pastor Catches Vision for Kingdom Fullness:
"God desires true diversity. Not heaven on earth, minus women. True diversity, not diversity we are comfortable with. Remaining comfortable doesn't benefit the church, the lost, or God. I'm looking at everything new. What was easy and available is not what God is calling me to. As brothers, we must call leaders who are women to the tables we sit at. They are God's tables, not ours. We need to find ways to be present, listen, grow in proximity, be confident in Christ. The Holy Spirit is making the way. I am fortunate enough to witness it and be invited into what God is already doing. It's time." – Rev. Jervie Windom

---

What is the cost of trading the promises of the Holy Spirit for bureaucracy or the illusion of security during cultural change? The cost isn't just the tally of women in ministry who "dropped off the radar," though that is a deep cost. Trading away our ordained women ignores our beautiful history. But trading the power and promises of the Holy Spirit betrays the anointing we claim. And while I grieve both, it's trading the promises of God that should break our hearts for the body of Christ.

Where is God asking us to see past the presenting symptom of a divide between women and men? Is the Holy Spirit prompting you or convicting you about something right now, today? Are there cracks between what you believe and how you live? Allowing God to realign our attitudes, actions, and loves will always result in a life lived more and more consistently with who God is and who God created us to be.

Not one of us lives a flawlessly consistent life.

But God cannot take us where we need to go if we do not first acknowledge where we have fallen short.

Where our movement has fallen short.

Where we have fallen short as individuals, leaders, and denominations, neglecting our call to live as a beacon of hope to the world in the design God intends for the body of Christ.

There are times in my life when the Holy Spirit convicts my heart of attitudes and assumptions I need to repent of, confess, and lament. It's never comfortable, but I don't want to settle for less than the full promises of God.

The Holy Spirit is restless to pour out on the body of Christ; none of us can hide from what English poet Francis Thompson called "the hound of heaven." When we hear a prophetic voice like Seth C. Rees, it can feel like a splash of cold water; but no one, woman or man, escapes the Holy Spirit, the "hound of heaven."

Rees seems to have known that in his bones. If God is the one chasing us down, why run?

If we're determined to escape, maybe we need the voice of an "earthquaker" to startle us toward God's persistent call. Maybe God is calling up earthquakers who aren't content with a tamed "hound."

Come, Holy Spirit, hound of heaven; pour out Your incomparably great grace and power.

Chapter Five Reflection & Discussion Questions

By Rev. Dr. Tamar Eisenmann, Lead Pastor,
Caring Community Church, MI

"I can't be the leader I'm supposed to be unless you are the leader you are supposed to be." These words from my husband rerouted our marriage and ministry.

I grew up a pastor's kid in a loving, Christian home. The domestic role never really appealed to me, but I tried to play it anyway. When I got married, I assumed my husband was the "head of the home." I waited for him to envision the next steps and make most of the decisions—just like my dad had done. But my husband is more like my mom, gifted in faith and perseverance no matter how discouraging things may be. And that's my husband: mind hard-wired to the present, reading the room, and doing what's necessary.

Early in our church-planting adventure, I always waited for him to realize what I already knew needed to be done. I became frustrated that he wasn't stepping up to be the head of our home and ministry. I could see he felt more and more like a failure. Since he couldn't lead in the way I expected, he increasingly stopped trying.

Eventually, he told me, "I can't be the leader I'm supposed to be unless you are the leader you are supposed to be." He challenged me to stop hiding behind him and become the leader God created me to be— someone who is constantly thinking about the future, who sees the way forward, and is gifted to communicate it.

While I sometimes get overwhelmed thinking about all that needs to be done, my husband doesn't. He leads by example, finding the faith and energy to keep moving forward while encouraging me to do so. Since we've accepted the unique ways that God gifted us to lead, we now enjoy unity, peace, and joy in our marriage and ministry we never had before.

When Christians insist on male headship, we devalue women who are gifted leaders, but we also devalue men who are gifted in ways besides leadership strategy and communication.

I've talked with men who drifted away from church because they could not live up to the leadership style their complementarian pastor modeled and taught. Usually, these men excel at solving problems with their hands. They serve selflessly, work diligently, and protect their families fiercely—including their wives' dreams.

One man told me, "I love my wife's dreams and plans for our future. Without her, my life would be so boring!" Another man told me, "According to the way my pastor preaches male headship, I'm not much of a man. I've never wanted to be the vocal, upfront type. I'm the 'come alongside and get-it-done type.'" To which I responded, "That's exactly the Holy Spirit's leadership type!"

In Genesis 1:26-28, God commands both man and woman to rule. Only when we focus on conforming ourselves to the image of Christ can we fulfill the mission of the church, in whom there is neither Jew nor Greek, slave nor free, male or female, but we are all one body with Christ Jesus as our head.

Discussion Questions

1. At the beginning of the chapter, we reviewed part of the heritage of women leading in Wesleyan/holiness denominations. Was any of that history new to you?

2. Were you surprised to see that at one time in a holiness denomination, at least 30% of ministers were women? What would that look like in your district now?

3. *Both the Daytons' paper and the Haines' research mention a shift away from ministry in impoverished or rural contexts, and both commented on how social pressure impacted the number of women in ministry. Did it surprise you to learn holiness churches used to be known for being "on the wrong side of the tracks"? If your congregation meets in a church building, what kind of area is it located in? How does your church engage with people in your county who are poor?*

4. *Have you heard the terms "complementarian" and "egalitarian" before? Are you surprised that Wesleyan/holiness biblical scholarship celebrates an egalitarian model of Christian marriage? Notice your response to this subject, and invite the Holy Spirit into any areas where you notice discomfort, relief, fear, frustration, or freedom.*

This Week

Take 15 minutes to pray for your denomination and district, thanking God for the ministry of women who planted churches and preached in your region long before you were alive. Ask the Holy Spirit for fearlessness in reaching out to people our Wesleyan/holiness movement used to be known for loving.

Consider ordering Celebrate Our Daughters: 150 Years of Women in Wesleyan Ministry *by Maxine L. Haines and Lee M. Haines (Wesleyan Publishing House) and look for towns or states you're familiar with. How can you share some of the stories and places relevant to your region that are mentioned in this resource?*

CHAPTER SIX

Dissecting Resistance to Kingdom Fullness

"Most merciful God, we confess that we have sinned
against you in thought, word, and deed,
by what we have done, and by what we have left undone.
We have not loved you with our whole heart; we have not
loved our neighbors as ourselves… " Confession of Sin
(Holy Eucharist Rite II), Book of Common Prayer[1]

What do you do when medical symptoms pop up, but imaging limitations fail to reveal the cause? When nothing definitive shows up on an X-ray, CT scan, or MRI? If testing doesn't reveal the problem but a doctor suspects something is wrong, they may opt to perform surgery only to discover a surprise, like a hidden cancerous tumor pressing into an organ.

Sometimes when there are symptoms of dysfunction, the cause lies below the surface; only surgery reveals the underlying problem. When we discover how something is going wrong, whether a smashed ankle that appeared "normal" on an x-ray or a hidden tumor pressing against a vital organ, then we can begin working toward repair, reset, and release.

In our shared life in the body of Christ, sometimes we see symptoms: some of the reasons *why* our Wesleyan/holiness movement settled for a church culture lacking women in lead pastor and denominational roles, for example.

But to find the mechanics of *how* it happened, let's take a closer look. How did the newly merged Wesleyan Church and other Wesleyan/holiness denominations lose so many pastors who were women? Anecdotally, it is clear there is a disproportionate gap between the number of women who complete part or all their ministerial training and the number of women active in formal positions of pastoral ministry. In denominations like my own, inconsistent reporting mechanisms make it challenging to track specific data, but those who invest in training ministerial candidates can attest to the reality of attrition among ministerial candidates who are women. Let's look under the surface.

What We Have Left Undone: Lost Resumes

One time, a friend shared her experience from years ago as a ministry student at a Wesleyan/Holiness university. At the time, the religious professors were supportive of women studying for ministry, but all the full-time professors in the department were male. A professor arranged a meeting with a top denominational leader and ministerial students who were women. The denominational leader was gracious and attempted to encourage students and highlight ways they might be able to get experience using their training and gifts. But the professor grew more and more restless until he burst out, "then why do district superintendents keep telling me not to send them the résumés of our female students? One told me, 'don't send me any more women, my churches won't consider them!'" The professor continued to fume with righteous indignation; at the time, there wasn't much the denominational leader could say in response.

It was an intense exchange, and yet the denominational leader and professor both supported the ordination of women for pastoral leadership. The professor took the step of proactive advocacy and arranged the meeting. In the context of this supportive setting, an informal bureaucratic challenge was identified and named: an essential step before the challenge itself could be addressed.

In practice, district superintendents asked professors for résumés of graduating ministerial students. Professors would respond, sharing the résumés of young men and women alike. And then superintendents sometimes communicated that résumés from students who were women were unnecessary or even unwelcome, either from the superintendent's preference or congregational resistance. Ideally, superintendents persist in sharing résumés from women with congregations, seizing the opportunity to celebrate biblical and denominational values and history. (Though if local board leaders were asked, maybe they would counter that superintendents rarely share résumés from women.)

This kind of mechanic can take years to bring to the surface until a particular person in a particular meeting happens to name it explicitly. Receiving, acknowledging, and sharing résumés is the kind of process we usually take for granted. We may assume that leaders exercise discernment regarding congregational "fit" only insofar as it relates to full or part-time, spiritual gifts and congregational personality, but not demographics.

It takes energy to make processes transparent, and it is not always easy, but it may be easier than standing in front of a room of students while women with four years' worth of student debt learn superintendents of Wesleyan/holiness denominations don't want to see their résumés. Several years before the professor's encounter described above, former General Superintendent of The Wesleyan Church Dr. Lee Haines addressed this very dynamic in strong, specific words: "District superintendents must not use the reluctance of…lay people in local churches as a cop-out in this matter [women in pastoral leadership]. If we exercise the strong leadership for this part of our work that we do in others, we can turn the tide."[2]

"What We Have Left Undone": When Delays Are No Longer Plausible

It can be challenging to name the mechanics of leveraging processes, delays, administrative omissions, unannounced last-minute changes to requirements, and paperwork. *For one thing, obstacles often appear in the context of working relationships that are not outwardly hostile.* Sometimes the mechanics play out in the context of friendly dynamics. While it can be hard, at least obstacles that emerge in collegial environments can be handled in the context of good-faith relationships. In those situations, if practices or processes are problematic, they exist among leaders who are willing to listen and who are genuinely invested in improving broken processes.

It is also challenging to name mechanics when they exist in a bureaucratic structure: the paperwork, policies, and procedures of church life. Administrative and clerical processes are already prone to genuine error or oversight. But procedures can be expedited or delayed, depending on who you're working with and their point of view.

When I first began pursuing ordination, I needed someone to sign a couple of basic forms. The person whose signatures were required agreed to sign my paperwork. "Great!" I thought.

I waited.

I followed up and waited some more.

After weeks had passed, I asked again.

After multiple inquiries, I ended up waiting for months.

Delays that seemed unnecessary but believable at first eventually stretched into a clear message. Officially, I'd been told I'd have what I needed to pursue ordination.

I never got it.

Eventually, I continued without the signatures, moving on to a more supportive environment.

The "me" of today would approach that situation differently. At the time, it took me off-guard. I heard a "yes," but unnecessary, ongoing delays became hurdles, and a hurdle is a soft "no."

Sometimes, there are plausible reasons. Everyone gets busy; paperwork genuinely gets lost in the shuffle or spam folder; inherited processes can be unnecessarily complicated. *That's not personal, it's just administrative life.*

At the same time, small decisions hold a lot of power: decisions like the choice to prioritize paperwork or drop it to the bottom of a to-do list indefinitely. If you've watched a meeting ordered by "parliamentary procedure," you know the power of a vote to "table" something—to delay it indefinitely until further notice. "Tabling" a matter avoids a "yes" or "no" vote; it avoids direct conflict in the short term. In American sports terms, it's like punting the football.

At the administrative level, "tabling" something or someone can look like inaction, passivity, or omission. It might look like ignoring résumés from women and sharing résumés from men when congregations are searching for a new pastor. Indefinite delays or omissions that accumulate are exhausting to navigate; they wear down ministerial candidates. Eventually, some women find other avenues to pursue their calling; some leave ministry for a season or altogether.

When actions for one group (like ministerial candidates who are women) fail to match efforts taken for another group (like ministerial candidates who are men), we are quietly committing the sin of omission: seeing the good we are called to do and neglecting to do it. It is the sin of leaving out. It's not done from genuine discernment but from habit or preference. It's neglecting to love our neighbors as ourselves. It's watching the ball go out of bounds without trying to stop it.

Short-term, administrative obstacles will always happen; no process, software, or person is perfect! But when intentional decisions tweak the flow of processes in ways that delay believers from pursuing God's call, these stumbling blocks aren't carried out "in good faith."

Good faith efforts are essential on all our parts when we're living God's vision for the body of Christ, extending trust as we co-labor together.

What We Have Done: From Quiet Hurdles to Loud Prejudice

Using administrative processes to delay or discourage someone from pursuing ministry is an indirect way of disagreeing with your denomination's heritage and theological position. It can be a quiet administrative protest (one affecting real people and with real consequences for reaching real lost people). Sometimes it is done without the knowledge of others, sometimes it is done with a wink.

In one situation, a woman ordained in a Wesleyan/holiness denomination was working in a compensated church staff position. When the senior pastor announced he was retiring, the search committee unanimously voted to recommend the woman on staff for the senior pastor position. However, when the district superinten-dent was informed, the DS intervened, responding that he didn't share the discernment of the search committee in the matter. He recommended she pursue an unpaid staff position at a different church and advised the committee to invite a particular male candi-date for the senior pastor position. Uncertain how to proceed, the committee acquiesced to the superintendent and invited the other candidate, eventually hiring the other candidate to become senior pastor. The woman who had been considered for the senior pastor role did not pursue the unpaid position at the other church. She is still following God's call and is active in pastoral ministry, but she is no longer in a Wesleyan/holiness denomination. Her ministry is the kingdom's gain, regardless; but her exit is a loss to our Wes-leyan/holiness spheres.

My sisters of color sometimes face louder, explicit obstacles when following God's call to pastoral ministry. Along with unspoken hurdles, there are times when individual congregations place very clear "road closed" signs, like those encountered by this ordained minister, who wrote of her recent experience in 2017: "One pasto-ral position I applied for yielded a call from a board member who asked me if I knew I was a black woman. 'We aren't looking for a woman, and certainly not a black woman,' the caller said. I am not sure how I was supposed to know that, especially since that infor-mation wasn't in the job announcement."[3]

That certainly wasn't a quiet or indirect hurdle.

Church, what are we doing?

How is this God-honoring?

God is calling us to live kingdom fullness, but interactions like that are designed to discourage, wound, and humiliate. Church to church, district to district, denomination to denomination, how can we be salt and light until we have repented with fasting and prayer for God's forgiveness? How can we genuinely embrace kingdom fullness before asking the forgiveness of pastors like our sisters in Christ?

The prayer of confession includes the phrase, "We have sinned against you in thought, word, and deed…" Her experience illustrates how sin in thought—derogatory thoughts and attitudes about women and people of color—can lead to sinning in words like derogatory speech that outright rejects an anointed minister without even meeting her or hearing her preach, without openness to the Holy Spirit to see if her gifts could be just what God knew would bless that congregation and community.

It's a serious matter to tell God that even if someone were the perfect pastoral fit for their church, even if their gifts were tailor-made for the context, the congregation would not accept a Spirit-filled leader of another race or an anointed leader who was a woman. This is not a posture shaped by the inspired Word of God. We need to take a long look at what shapes our values when our values fall short of that glorious vision of heaven in Revelation, "After this I looked, and there before me was a great multitude that no one could count, from every nation, tribe, people, and language, standing before the throne and before the Lamb. They were wearing white robes and were holding palm branches in their hands. And they cried out in a loud voice: 'Salvation belongs to our God, who sits on the throne, and to the Lamb'" (Rev. 7:9-10).

This is scripture's portrait of the kingdom of God! This is the fullness of Pentecost. This is heaven.

But with experiences like the ones shared above, some clergywomen know if they leave their denomination, it won't be considered a loss. This worsens the attrition of educated, trained, and equipped pastors. Rudeness and prejudice grieve the Holy Spirit and fall short of scripture and our Wesleyan/holiness values.

Whether or not your denomination considers it a loss, sisters, God sees you. God hears you. Together, all of us are called to respond to the Holy Spirit's creative, joyful work bestowing gifts on the body of Christ for the building up of the body, no matter what context or setting or denomination we find ourselves in.

For all pastors, brothers and sisters alike: when you choose to step out and answer God's call, when you sacrifice in obedience to Christ and you face discourtesy, disrespect, or dismissal, hear this: our God is the God Who Sees. It was a woman who gave God that name: "she gave this name to the Lord who spoke to her: 'You are the God who sees me,' for she said, 'I have now seen the One who sees me'" (Gen. 16:13). All pastors, remember that when you feel most invisible, God sees you. God witnesses our struggles and comes alongside us. After all, if he sees the sparrows and takes care of them (Matt. 6:26), how much more does he care for us? Any pastor, man or woman, can feel like they've fallen through the cracks. Together, God calls us to celebrate each other as we build up the body of Christ.

Come, Holy Spirit: when we fall through the cracks, remind us we belong to You and that You take joy in us, rejoicing over us with singing (Zeph. 3:17).

Chapter Six Reflection & Discussion Questions

By Rev. Tanya Nace, M.A.; CEO,
World Hope International, Canada

Lord, we seek Your wisdom as we navigate these symptoms and reasons for division. We seek unity and love as we take the necessary steps to work hand-in-hand for Your kingdom. We desire to see Your kingdom come here on earth as it is in heaven. Amen.

Discussion Questions

1. *It can be easier to recognize the symptoms of a problem more than the problem itself. Through prayer, what symptoms can you identify? Can you name the reason(s) these symptoms may exist in the kingdom circles you belong to? After considering these symptoms, how would you diagnose the problem?*

2. *Are you transparent with yourself about the symptoms that you see? Are you transparent with others about the symptoms seen?*

3. *I invite you to pray with a Psalm 139:23-24 posture: "Search me, God, and know my heart; test me and know my anxious thoughts. See if there is any offensive way in me and lead me in the way everlasting." How can you go before the Lord and ask him to give you direction in naming these challenges in a loving and anointed manner?*

4. *What types of actions could you take to break down walls of administrative, cultural, and social roadblocks that keep women from gaining access to lead pastor roles in the church,*

thereby creating more access to leadership roles and a pipeline of leadership and pastoral development?

5. *How do you envision brothers and sisters working and servant-leading together in kingdom fullness within your ministry context? In your local church leadership? In your district or denominational leadership? In your internship and residency programs?*

This Week

Whether you're a church member, pastor, or denominational leader, look up the ministerial candidate process in two or three districts or conferences in your denomination. Are you able to find the process on the relevant websites? Is the process the same for each district? Is it clear and easy to follow? Take ten minutes to pray for all those currently in the ordination process and for the church members, pastors, and district leaders who give time and energy to serve on boards tasked with the burden and blessing of discerning candidates' pastoral readiness.

CHAPTER SEVEN

Living Surrendered

"He withdrew about a stone's throw beyond them, knelt down and prayed, 'Father, if you are willing, take this cup from me; yet not my will, but yours be done.' An angel from heaven appeared to him and strengthened him. And being in anguish, he prayed more earnestly, and his sweat was like drops of blood falling to the ground"
(Luke 22:41-44).

"Therefore, if you are offering your gift at the altar and there remember that your brother or sister has something against you, leave your gift there in front of the altar. First go and be reconciled to them; then come and offer your gift"
(Matt. 5:23-24).

Sometimes in hospital settings, patients find themselves in very vulnerable moments, requiring assistance with personal needs. But it's impossible to be a good nurse and avoid frank conversations with patients. If I avoided asking patients potentially uncomfortable questions, I couldn't provide them with good care. When I stopped working as a nurse full-time to enter pastoral ministry, frank conversations were still necessary sometimes. In ministry and in medicine, hard conversations include acknowledging and naming difficult things.

When is it easier to acknowledge your vulnerability and dependence on others: when you're wearing a hospital gown, or when you're wearing a necktie or high heels? Patients may get mad that they need help, but there comes a point when even challenging patients come face to face with their limitations. Everyone handles loss of control in different ways; it's why doctors and nurses so often make difficult patients! They're used to being in charge. But the illusion of control disappears quickly when you must accept help using the restroom. It's hard putting your best foot forward while you're wearing a hospital gown. Accepting the situation with grace, humility, gratitude, and good humor will usually be the best response. After all, you may not like being in the hospital, but your triple-bypass doesn't really care whether you like it or not, and refusing to accept help will only delay recovery and healing.

Grace, humility, gratitude, good humor: all these are helpful attitudes and practices when it comes to surrender. Jesus shows us the way: before he was on the cross having a hard conversation with John about taking responsibility for caring for his widowed mother Mary, Gethsemane came first.

If you've ever been to church services where there's a healthy practice of "altar calls" to respond genuinely to the Holy Spirit's conviction, you probably know surrender doesn't start at the altar, it starts in the argument you have with God in your seat. Maybe you remember going forward to pray to accept Christ as the rescuer or Lord of your life. Maybe you've responded in a service when someone preached, and you knew the Holy Spirit was calling you to ministry. There are times speakers will misuse those kinds of settings to try to manipulate a response, but that doesn't change the fact that sometimes we know God is moving and want to respond. It's a gift to our kids and elders, new believers, and saints, when our leaders don't just worship in front of others but are willing to be called to new surrender in front of others. Nothing keeps us humble like choosing to let the Holy Spirit convict us in front of each other.

Do you remember a particular moment when the Holy Spirit nudged you? Maybe you knelt at your grandma's couch or responded to a sermon or felt the joy of worshiping with the body of Christ. Maybe God met you at the bottom of a bottle, in a jail cell, or during a sleep-deprived night caring for a sick loved one. Maybe you wanted to get baptized, or you knew you needed to allow Jesus to be Lord of your loves and life, not just your rescuer. Maybe you sensed a terrifying or joyful leap of your spirit when God whispered or thundered a call to serve and lead through ministry.

Are you still surrendered?

This side of heaven, there will always be more to surrender.

I wish I could offer a comfortable shortcut. But like Jesus knew in Gethsemane, the only way is through.

If you come forward to offer a sacrifice—like your life, as a response to God's call—and there, you remember… then leave your gift, go, make it right, make peace, find alignment… then return and offer your life to God.

There is surrender in the going forward to offer yourself for ministry.

There is surrender in the remembering.

There is surrender in the choice to leave your gift.

There is surrender in making peace, restitution, and realignment.

There is surrender in the return.

There is surrender in the offering.

Sometimes doctors make the most difficult patients—and sometimes church leaders have the hardest time surrendering to the Holy Spirit, because we mistake proximity to the sacred with loving and obeying Jesus Christ.

If you avoid surrendering your ego to Jesus, how will you find the humility to learn from someone else?

If you're defensive with the Holy Spirit, how will you find the grace to be vulnerable with someone who's human?

It's much easier to enter hard conversations with humans when you've already allowed God to have hard conversations with you. When the Holy Spirit has convicted you about something, what trouble is apologizing to Sue in accounting, in comparison? None of us will ever be more vulnerable with each other than we are with God almighty. If God's grace transforms vulnerability with God into safety with God, then grace can transform openness, humility, and vulnerability with each other into anointed space ready for the Holy Spirit to propel into breathtaking kingdom fullness.

How did Jesus live? We don't find either belligerence or avoidance characterizing his conversations. The Gospels show us a range of interactions:

- Jesus stayed silent sometimes (studiously tracing in the dirt when a woman was caught in adultery; during his own arrest and questioning).

- Jesus demonstrated and expressed holy anger (braiding a whip to drive out those profiting from poor believers; the "woes" to the Pharisees).

- Jesus had hard conversations in front of others (the rich young ruler) but also in private (talking with Nicodemus out of public view at night).

- Jesus grieved over the ways people treated each other when they rejected God's mercy (when his feet were anointed with oil; when he wept over Jerusalem).

- Jesus saw others' motives and aimed for the heart of the matter, whether the conversation was about which disciple was greatest or whether it was right to pay taxes owed to Caesar.
- Jesus always had eyes for individual people, despite large crowds: Zacchaeus up a tree, Mary learning from his teaching while Martha prepared dinner, parents bringing their kids to be blessed.
- Jesus knew when people weren't asking questions in good faith; he saw when they were trying to trap him, trip him up, set him up, or bring him down.

Through all that, Jesus wasn't ever defensive. He was honest, sometimes confrontational, occasionally angry. But Jesus was never petty, resentful, condescending, or callous. Self-protective instincts make it hard to listen deeply; Jesus was wise, but he had no need to posture or try to put his best foot forward.

If God's grace transforms vulnerability with God into safety with God, then grace can transform openness, humility, and vulnerability with each other into anointed space ready for the Holy Spirit to propel into breathtaking kingdom fullness.

It's hard for the Holy Spirit to work when our defensiveness is alert and engaged. All pastors and church leaders, men or women, can grow protective shells against criticism and comparison. Even if you know there's a difference between growing a thick skin and a hard heart, it can take godly counsel, prayer, and time to tell which one you have. Sometimes prayer gently melts away the brittle pieces as the Holy Spirit carries your grief and lament, walking you into forgiveness and peace.

For those who are tired or burned out, your shoulders may tense just thinking about some of the topics in chapters to come, preemptively picturing escalating conflict or painful criticism. I've had moments when I wanted nothing more than to avoid a difficult conversation. It's easy to imagine interactions going downhill; then we question whether it's even worth it. This is the toll discouragement takes: it's the temptation to not try.

There will always be times when we need to enter into hard conversations. Later in "Side by Side," we'll look at examples of the early church's struggle in working out shared life, even amid an incredible outpouring of the Holy Spirit. Then and now, none of us picks up a book or enters a conversation as a blank slate; we bring our experiences, wounds, fears, and personal and cultural expectations. Hopefully, you've come to a place where you're aware of the baggage you bring with you, and you've found encouragement through the gift of mentors, coaches, community, written resources, sound mental health care, and therapy. Good mental health professionals are a gift of grace as they live their vocation to equip the personal and relational flourishing of others.

If you're wrestling with surrender or just feel tense around some of these topics, sit for a moment; consider your responses to these questions.

- Have you looked forward to any chapters, skipping ahead, or delayed some?

- When you think about some chapters, do specific situations or people come to mind? If so, do you still have a strong emotional response to those circumstances or interactions?

- If you come from a background of abuse or one that makes building trust take extra time and intentionality, have you been able to begin building relationships with those co-laborers who continue to earn your trust?

- Are you noticing areas in your spirit where the Holy Spirit is prompting you to forgive someone else, or to ask forgiveness, or to forgive yourself for not handling something differently?

- Are there insights from Pete Scazzero's book *Emotionally Healthy Spirituality* that might be applicable as you engage with challenging chapters?

- While I approach these chapters through scriptural principles, I can only coach as a person from a particular place and time in history. That simply means that like our missionaries are deeply aware of, different cultures have different expectations, practices, and vocabulary for navigating subjects like conflict (see "Trust: How to Enter Hard Conversations"). If you have a different cultural background than I do, do some of your approaches to hard conversations differ from mine? What should we be aware of when *hard conversations* are also *cross-cultural interactions*, or when one of the participants is using a language that isn't their primary language?

These questions are worth our time, because none of us wants to be misunderstood. None of us wants to hurt someone's feelings. None of us wants to be labeled. None of us wants to be disrespectful or appear so. None of us wants to make things worse in the process of trying to make them better.

Absorb this good word from scripture: "for the Spirit God gave us does not make us timid, but gives us power, love and self-discipline" (2 Tim. 1:7). Surrendered to Christ, through the Holy Spirit, you and I have the opportunity to strengthen our leadership and our witness. God empowers us to steward our working relationships by prayerfully discerning when new expressions of trust may be built, maintained, and expanded. When power comes from the Holy Spirit, it's always accompanied by self-giving love and mindful discipline. As we co-labor, we can walk confidently—not in our own perspectives, status, or ability, but in the trustworthiness of the One who calls and equips us for every good work.

All of us need to surrender to God's grace if we want to interact under pressure with kindness, humility, and honesty. All of us need wisdom, discerning when to confront and when to release. The more we engage with scripture, rest in God through prayer, and remain open to the wisdom of those investing in our growth, the more space we give the Holy Spirit to show us things we hadn't realized about ourselves.

Surrender is the only way forward.

Holy Spirit, give us the strength to surrender it all–for the sake of the lost, to the glory of God. Amen.

Chapter Seven Reflection & Discussion Questions

By Rev. Dr. "Umfundisi" Jim Lo, Director of World Missions at Churches of God Holiness; Professor Emeritus and Former Dean of Chapel of Indiana Wesleyan University

To share the love and message of Christ to those in the Caribbean, the Moravians of old sold themselves as slaves to obtain passage to this land so far from them. Missionaries used to pack their meager belongings in coffins since they realized that death was a real possibility. These are examples of total surrender.

While in China a few summers ago, I heard about young men who, because they are Christians, have been beaten and thrown into jail. Often their jail sentences last up to three years. But instead of seeing their time of imprisonment as a waste, some of these young men have begun to preach God's word to the other inmates. One shared, "the government thought they could stop me from starting up a church ... but little do they realize that there is a church right in their own prisons."

Some of these Christian young people, upon being released from prison, will go home for a few weeks, spend time with their families, and then boldly begin to preach the Gospel again, knowing they will be put back into prison. The wife of one imprisoned man said, "I am willing to totally surrender myself to God and his will and to make the sacrifice of having my husband imprisoned ... especially when it means that he can go back and disciple those who have come into a relationship with Jesus. No sacrifice is too great for Christ!" She understands the meaning of total surrender... the act of giving God the blank check of your life and letting him fill it out.

In this chapter, Pastor Katie has admonished us to totally surrender ourselves to God. This is not easy to do. But the blessings will be stupendous!

Discussion Questions

1. *Can you point to a time when God asked you to acknowledge and name difficult things in your life? What were some of those things? Did you accept God's questions to you with a humble attitude or defensively?*

2. *When you feel you have lost control...*
   a. *What happens to your attitude?*
   b. *What happens to your actions?*
   c. *What happens to your relationship with... God? Yourself? Others?*

3. *When someone shares "constructive criticism" to you, are you open to it?*

4. *Pastor Katie wrote, "Grace, humility, gratitude, good humor: all these are helpful attitudes and practices when it comes to surrender." Practically, how would you describe the following:*
   a. *"surrendered grace"*
   b. *"surrendered humility"*
   c. *"surrendered gratitude"*
   d. *"surrendered good humor"*

5. *Jesus Christ models for us what having hard conversations with someone should look like. What are some things Jesus did when confronting someone?*

6. *Why is it important for us to surrender our "ego" to God?*

7. *How can you lovingly "confront" someone to help that individual to go "deeper" with Christ?*

8. *How can being surrendered to God strengthen one's leadership and one's witness to others?*

9. *Pastor Katie writes, "Surrender is the only way forward." Practically, how does her statement relate to where you are presently?*

10. *What does God use to show us things we hadn't realized about ourselves to help us grow spiritually and as leaders? (Pastor Katie suggested four things.)*

11. *What do you need to surrender to God? Take time to reflect and act on this step now.*

This Week

Intentionally create some margin in your schedule so that by yourself, with a friend, or in gathered worship, you give the Holy Spirit time to sort through your heart and show you what needs to be surrendered.

CHAPTER EIGHT

How We Steward Kingdom-Full Vocation

*"Therefore, if you have any encouragement from being
united with Christ, if any comfort from his love, if any
common sharing in the Spirit, if any tenderness and
compassion, then make my joy complete by being
like-minded, having the same love, being one in spirit and
of one mind. Do nothing out of selfish ambition or vain
conceit. Rather, in humility value others above yourselves,
not looking to your own interests but each of you to the
interests of the others" (Phil. 2:1-4).*

God has given us this beautiful commission: to go and make disciples. Part of that means stewarding vocation well by entering spaces with the goal of following Jesus' example in how we approach the disciples who are already there. We are making disciples through the power of the Holy Spirit with the love of Jesus, not dismantling disciples with attitudes and language that tear down, alienate, or grieve the Spirit of God in our midst.

No one speaks with perfect charity all the time. I don't know a single human who hasn't said something careless from time to time, myself certainly included! But the Spirit empowers each of us to grow in becoming Christlike, to grow in how we steward our calling. We each have the opportunity to ask the Holy Spirit how we are stewarding our vocation through our words, habits, and attitudes. This becomes increasingly essential as we grow in leadership and responsibility. As Rev. Dr. Tammy Dunahoo, Executive Dean of Portland Seminary and former general supervisor of The Foursquare Church puts it, "as God graciously makes your circle of influence larger, be sure to ask him to make your circle of accountability larger just the same."[1]

Beginning to Mend: Mindfully Engaging Communication Habits

"I'm sorry, I shouldn't be speaking like that in front of you. The group of pastors before you were all men. Where I come from, we don't speak in front of women like that."

In a conference breakout session, I was the only pastor in the room who was a woman. Within the first ten minutes, the speaker stopped to apologize to me three times. I finally asked why he kept apologizing; he explained the group before mine had been all-male. The speaker was genuinely trying to be polite and considerate by apologizing. But his presentations to the all-male groups included comments he was uncomfortable saying in front of women.

How we communicate matters if we want to "do no harm" and steward our vocations well. Words matter, not because potential participants are delicate or over-sensitive, needing protection. Nurses hear it all: I wasn't shocked by anything I heard, even if I wasn't expecting to hear it in a faith-based conference breakout session.

The problem wasn't that the speaker struggled to adapt his comments to a different audience. If comments aren't suitable when women are present in the room, then they probably aren't professional in any room. Our words should be fitting and expansive enough to honor those present or anyone who enters the room.

This isn't true just for off-color jokes or stories. Communicating with pre-emptive welcome stretches further than that. If it is possible you'll be in contexts where "pastors and spouses" wording is needed rather than "pastors and wives," you can start practicing using "pastors and spouses" as your default wording all the time, regardless of the setting. On the flip side, if you'd never hear a speaker introduced with, "Our next speaker is a male pastor…" then there's no reason to introduce a speaker with, "Our next speaker is a female pastor…"

In something as simple as wording, we can bear witness to the goodness of God, who calls women and men to preach the Gospel. We can bear witness to each other's calling by celebrating each other's task of proclaiming the good news.

Why do our words matter? Our speech matters because we honor God when we honor God's creation, and every human being bears the image of God. Jesus laughed, drank, ate, and participated in celebrations—and always treated each person with simplicity and dignity.

So even when we don't get it right, it's valuable to pause, acknowledge where we are falling short and trying to grow new habits, and then ask some trusted peers to help keep us accountable to our goals. This is part of our sanctification.

Followers of Christ are called to bear witness to God's goodness with our lives and with our words. When we bear witness with our words, we're not just bearing witness to unbelievers. We're bearing witness to each other, by how we treat each other and speak and act.

If we believe that "where two or three are gathered together," God "is in the midst of them," then any time we gather, we can submit our attitudes, habits, and words to Christ. One way we surrender our attitudes, words, and interactions to the Lordship of Christ is by paying attention. We can't surrender what we don't notice.

The day my presence alerted a speaker to his default stories, humor, and language, it had been assumed:

- The audience of pastors would be all-male.
- The comments were appropriate to the context and professionally fitting as long as only men were present.

Rather than make these assumptions, what if church leaders operate from a different default setting? What if we choose to assume:

- Since God calls a variety of people to ministry, we should expect diversity in our audience (and should grieve if our audience doesn't reflect it).
- Since habits are easy to make and hard to break, our language should be consistent regardless of setting, circumstance, or audience.
- Since iron sharpens iron, language in professional settings should be a model of respect for other people, whether specific groups are present or not.
- Since no one gets it right all the time, we as speakers will be quick to listen, quick to apologize, quick to learn, and quick to do it differently next time, because we don't want anything to distract from the mission or from our witness.

Do church leaders and speakers need to take themselves seriously all the time? That's not what I mean at all! We can be intentional and show respect with the language and content we use without taking ourselves too seriously.

In fact, it's hard to take yourself too seriously if you practice the discipline of apologizing. It's healthy to be able to laugh at ourselves. Asking for forgiveness keeps us all humbly self-aware. "Therefore each of you must put off falsehood and speak truthfully to your neighbor, for we are all members of one body. 'In your anger do not sin': Do not let the sun go down while you are still angry, and do not give the devil a foothold" (Eph. 4:25-27). When you practice the habit of asking forgiveness from someone you've offended or wronged (intentionally or unintentionally), you don't give room for the enemy to cause division.

No church leader wants to miss the opportunity to connect with others for kingdom fullness by using wording, language, or humor that belittles or alienates other people. If we humiliate or exclude, we're missing the opportunity for others to entrust us with their stories of God's unique work in their lives.

When church leaders speak, teach, and preach, we are welcoming each other into the presence of the Holy Spirit, asking God to meet with us and to communicate the heart of Jesus to us and through us. If we keep that in mind, it's easier to let go of habits that don't serve us well, easier to pursue new attitudes and practices as we celebrate each other's vocation in the beauty of kingdom fullness.

Beginning to Mend: Mindfully Engaging Learning Habits

Sometimes, we steward vocation well by paying attention to what's present in our words and interactions. Sometimes, we steward vocation well by noticing what or who is absent. To explore who might be missing, consider: who do you learn from, take instruction from, or choose to gain insight from? Do you consider yourself teachable? Here's another question: who are you willing to teach, instruct, or share insights with? Do you consider yourself comfortable exercising leadership? Have you worked to grow in exercising your gifts?

If my brothers who are reading this answered comfortably in your hearts that you're willing to learn from, take instruction from, or gain insight from a woman in church leadership, then let's move to these follow-up questions:

How do you practice following a woman in leadership?

Can you name a woman who mentors or coaches you?

If in practice you aren't currently able to work with a woman in leadership or you can't currently name a woman mentoring you, is this an opportunity to evaluate who your mentors, supervisors, or coaches are? Are you open to praying over and pursuing a greater range of voices speaking into your life? God wants to unleash kingdom fullness into our shared congregational life, but the Holy Spirit is also eager to pour out the blessing of kingdom fullness into the individual lives of leaders as well.

In the past few years, I had the privilege of interviewing a church leader for whom I continue to have great respect. At one point I asked, "if you don't mind, I'd like to ask—what are some names of leaders who are women, who you have chosen (not been assigned) to speak into your life and ministry?"

In that moment, he couldn't offer any names. But a few days later, he reached out to express appreciation for the question and the reflection it prompted. Godly church leaders can give dedicated support to women following God's call to pastoral ministry, yet still discover gaps in the ways women speak into their lives. Sometimes this is simply due to decades of attrition of women in all levels of leadership, but the challenge remains. If we value kingdom fullness, sometimes seeking out the leadership of women requires proactive intentionality.

Another way to steward vocation is evaluating the resources you engage with. What materials do you use in your church? Are there authors who don't share Wesleyan/holiness theology and heritage on women's ordination?

This might also take a different shape.

One day I spoke with a male colleague about habits that shape perspective and practices on women in leadership. He smiled and shared his own experience. Unlike many Wesleyan/holiness pastors who are men, he had experience with a woman in leadership who was his direct mentor. One day, she asked him to go to his bookshelves and bring her the books he owned written by women.

He was a little embarrassed at how short the stack of books was.

We have so many great books by Wesleyan Methodist church leaders, scholars, and pastors who are women! From books on ministry, leadership, and biblical studies, to resources on theology, doctrine, or small group studies, and many more subjects. If you believe God calls women to pastoral ministry and church leadership (or even if you're not sure yet), increase the number of books you read or listen to this year that have been written by pastors, scholars, and leaders who are women.

Beginning to Mend: Mindfully Engaging Leadership Habits

We can also steward the vocation of others by ensuring guests on a platform (and pastors who transfer from other traditions) know and embrace our Wesleyan/holiness theology and heritage of ordaining women. One leader I respect took bold steps to reassess an invitation to a speaker after discovering that the speaker did not support women in all roles of ministry. Others work to make sure women are invited to speak at conferences and gatherings. With the number of gifted, trained women at work across Wesleyan/holiness denominations, there is no need for discussion panels or podcasts to solely feature male guests.

Leaders also steward vocation well when we teach from our rich supply of resources developed by gifted and godly Wesleyan/holiness scholars. Some of these particularly give attention to the biblical foundations for egalitarian marriage. If church leaders and congregations neglect this topic or use resources that contradict our Wesleyan/holiness theology, we face an added challenge in communicating kingdom fullness.

There's another very practical way for leaders to steward God's calling on others. Many women encounter challenges in the ordination process due to difficulty finding congregations that will host their "field experience" or preaching requirements. Simply by communicating that your church is available to host practical experience, you remove hurdles for women trying to complete the ministerial training process.

While I was navigating the ordination process, I struggled to find congregations willing to host me as a guest speaker, where I could gain the preaching experience expected of ordination candidates and church planters. Finally, my husband and I started an informal "preaching club" with other ordination candidates, including several women who *also* hadn't been able to find pastors or congregations willing to welcome them to their pulpits. Some women invest a lot of time and energy into training for pastoral ministry, only to find they can't complete their field experience requirement because there are no pastors in their region who are willing to host them. If a pastor is hesitant to open the pulpit to ordination candidates in general, it might be reassuring to remember that ordination candidates meet regularly with district boards; there's no ordination candidate who's unvetted by a district.

Hosting an emerging preacher is such a simple way to pursue kingdom fullness! Do we truly value the gift of kingdom fullness the Lord has given to each of us: the gift of each other?

While I was navigating the ordination process, I struggled to find congregations willing to host me as a guest speaker, where I could gain the preaching experience expected of ordination candidates and church planters. Finally, my husband and I started an informal "preaching club" with other ordination candidates, including several women who also hadn't been able to find pastors or congregations willing to welcome them to their pulpits.

That question leads directly to another opportunity to ask how church leaders can steward the vocation of others. How can leaders proactively guide congregations in the direction of our Wesleyan/ holiness theology and heritage of celebrating the ordination of women?

Practically, for congregational systems of church government, stewarding the vocations of others may look like districts consistently including the résumés of women in the stack offered to church boards during pastoral transition or responding to communication from pastors who are women. It honors God's goodness when leaders celebrate scriptural texts like Acts 2, Galatians 3:28, and Revelation 7:9.

Beginning to Mend: Mindfully Engaging with Teams

As I coach pastors and provide training, I get to witness some of the beautiful ways God is moving and working. It's a blessing to watch leaders catch a vision for kingdom fullness. And sometimes pastors who are men have reached out requesting training for themselves and their teams.

It's refreshing to hear honest comments like, "I don't know *what I don't know*. But we have women in my church who are being called by God and who we want to raise up. How can we do that? What do I need to be looking for?"

These are the kinds of questions that lead to fruitful conversations, honest engagement, and space for God to move and work as men and women discover and live into their calling. It's exciting to see brothers and sisters partnering together for God's kingdom! When church leaders proactively search out ways to support and equip both men and women who are responding to God's call, it's an amazing vision of the body of Christ not only functioning but flourishing.

Come, Holy Spirit; empower us to steward each other's calling well.

Chapter Eight Reflection & Discussion Questions

By Rev. Zach Coffin, Director of Partnership for Kingswood
Learn; Consultant and Coach

In my early twenties, I had a pivotal moment that forever changed how I view the power of my words. During a routine executive team meeting at my church, the conversation among our predominantly male team turned into inappropriate joking, which, regrettably, I had come to see as normal and acceptable. I remember seeing the discomfort on our female pastor's face, but because I thought this was "behind-closed-door joking," I joined the banter.

After the meeting, the conviction of the Holy Spirit weighed heavily on me. I approached my female teammate to apologize, but what was I apologizing for? Was I apologizing because a woman heard the coarse joking or because the joking was ungodly, regardless of who was in the room?

Sadly, up until this point, I had never considered how coarse joking had little to do with who was in the room and who wasn't. My joking was ungodly and unholy. I apologized to my teammate, and her response only affirmed the unspoken burden she had carried. She said, "Zach, I know your heart and know you really didn't mean what you said. I have three boys; I know how this goes." At that moment, I felt absolved and thanked my teammate for her grace, but her comment, "I have parented three boys, I know how this goes," has never settled well.

The hard truth is that the people (including myself) in that executive pastoral team meeting were not "boys." We are supposed to be men who honor God in thought, word, and deed. That season of my life is one I grieve deeply and have sought forgiveness for from my teammates.

It has also become a crucial lesson in stewarding my words and walking in holiness no matter who is in the room. My words and joking should not get a "pass" just because of the gender or pastoral position represented in the room.

The joking I once dismissed as harmless fun was dishonoring to both God and my team. I no longer give myself a "pass" under the guise of humor or camaraderie. Instead, I strive to create an environment where my daughters—and anyone else, regardless of gender—could sit in on a meeting and feel respected, valued, included, and walk in holiness before the Lord.

This is a work of the Spirit that I am continuously submitting to, and it's one I hope will leave a lasting impact on the holiness people experience in my life.

Discussion Questions

1. Have you ever found yourself participating in conversations or humor that you later realized were inappropriate or ungodly? What did you do when you realized?

2. When apologizing for something you've said or done, do you find yourself focusing more on who was offended or on the nature of the words or actions themselves? Why do you think that is?

3. Have you ever excused your language or behavior because of the people present in the room? How might this differ from how you would act in front of other people?

4. What unspoken burdens do you think others might carry in your workplace or community due to the language or behavior of those around them? How can you help to lighten those burdens?

5. *Reflecting on your own experiences, from your perspective, have gender dynamics influenced the way you speak or act in different settings? How might these dynamics—whatever they are— shift toward proactive hospitality for anyone in the room?*

6. *What steps can you take to make sure everyone in your meetings feels respected, valued, and included? How can you ensure that your actions and words align with these values?*

7. *How do you plan to continue submitting your words and actions to the Holy Spirit? What specific changes or commitments are you willing to make to walk in greater holiness in your interactions with others?*

This Week

Look at the books on your shelves, the podcasts you listen to, the leaders you "follow" or subscribe to. Do the authors and leaders you learn from embody an Acts 2 anointing: women and men gathered in the upper room, people from different places and languages empowered by the Spirit to hear in their own language? Or do the authors and leaders you learn from resemble your own background, peer group, or neighborhood? Mindfully add some new authors, leaders, and pastors whose work may help you grow as you engage more fully with the Body of Christ.

CHAPTER NINE

Do No Harm: Healthy, Holy, Practical Alternatives to the BGR

Most merciful God,
we confess that we have sinned against you
in thought, word, and deed,
by what we have done,
and by what we have left undone.
We have not loved you with our whole heart;
we have not loved our neighbors as ourselves.
We are truly sorry and we humbly repent.
For the sake of your Son Jesus Christ,
have mercy on us and forgive us;
that we may delight in your will,
and walk in your ways,
to the glory of your Name. Amen.
                                    — *Book of Common Prayer*[1]

M any doctors are guided by a code for medical practice known as the Hippocratic oath—a code thousands of years old. The most famous part is summarized: "first, do no harm." It sounds simple and straightforward. When you begin to treat a patient, first make sure you don't do additional damage.

But this hasn't always been straightforward for medical practitioners. In the 1930s, a great new substance was developed to protect people from skin cancer: sunscreen! By the twenty-first century, some doctors started expressing concern that overeager parents were using an unnecessarily high SPF sunscreen on their babies. This can accidentally block children from absorbing vitamin D from sunlight, contributing to a rise in a disease called rickets. Rickets is caused by lack of vitamin D; it weakens a child's leg bones to the point they bow under the weight of their bodies.

In other words, the solution for one problem led to a new problem.

Even today in the medical profession, a lot of work is invested in constantly revising how to "do no harm" as treatments are developed. Before you can effectively pursue the goal of helping a patient get well, you first must discern which treatments might do more harm than good.

When the body of Christ shows signs of deficiency and dysfunction, what should guide our response? Let's look at a common practice often thought to be the only solution for one problem but that in practice creates a host of others. Throughout the Gospels and Acts, we see examples of how God calls men and women to collaborate for the kingdom with creativity and respect. We're called to steward our vocations and the vocations of our sisters and brothers well. Is the "Billy Graham rule" or other one-size-fits-all rules really the most effective way men and women in the church can "do no harm" while working together in the church? (After all, women and men worked together long before Rev. Graham was born.)

In training workshops, when I lead conversations on reassessing our relationship with the "Billy Graham rule" (simplified to the

BGR for the rest of the chapter), I find it's helpful to clarify what I *don't* mean. *I don't mean:*

- Pastors should throw away personal and professional guidelines, boundaries, or wisdom.

- Ministry colleagues should exercise the same set of practices for interactions with community and church members as they do ministerial colleagues.

- Pastors should ignore their spouse's perspectives.

- Slow, careful discernment in step with the Holy Spirit could never outwardly resemble elements of the BGR.

- That Billy Graham's ministry was insignificant or that he was wrong to follow a shared covenant guideline in his extremely rare situation.

- That the stakes are low for our witness, or that the trauma of devastated pastoral families, church families, and congregations doesn't matter.

Instead, let's ask *what it could look like if we live into kingdom fullness and steward our calling by honoring what Dr. Jo Anne Lyon refers to as "invisible boundaries" that frame how we relate to each other in healthy, holy ways.*

In the next sections, we'll consider the original scope of the BGR; ministry hurdles created by one-size-fits-all rules; the ineffectiveness of the BGR; the difference between visible rules and invisible boundaries; a refreshing look at how leaders practiced healthy boundaries without the BGR decades ago; and a practical example from a current church staff. With professionalism, emotionally healthy boundaries, self-awareness, and spiritual maturity, how might the Holy Spirit be calling us forward?

One Rule to Rule Them All

When a well-respected Baptist evangelist skyrocketed to fame in the 1940s and 1950s, he and several other ministers developed a simple code to live by to protect their integrity and reputations as pastors suddenly in the worldwide media spotlight. Rev. Graham traveled around the world away from home for months at a time, constantly photographed and followed by global paparazzi eager to find or manufacture "dirt" on the evangelist. In response to the intense attention, part of his shared code was the commitment not to meet alone with any woman other than his wife—what was later popularized by other pastors as the "Billy Graham rule." Late in life, Rev. Graham expressed regret that he'd been away from home so much while his children were growing up[2].

Rev. Graham found himself in an exceptionally rare situation. Few of us will ever find ourselves in his shoes under a global spotlight. And even fewer of us will ever find ourselves preaching to millions of people at once and answering interview questions from global reporters.

So why did the personal code of one famous evangelist become widespread among pastors around the United States? The original scope for this very personal commitment was limited and linked to several other shared commitments around ethical matters. Yet it's become nearly sacrilegious to suggest that mass adoption of this practice has been ineffective at best.

In all the conversations I have as a coach, I find men and women are looking for workable models of healthy engagement. Some groundwork for this is done when leaders proactively engage with sound resources on professional interpersonal communication building blocks like teamwork "soft skills," emotional intelligence, and self-awareness. Strengthening capacity in those competencies is valuable whether you're a dentist, drive-thru manager, or district superintendent[3] (or if you've had an interesting vocational journey, all of the above!).

Even so, this topic can cause men and women both to flinch; it's a discussion best approached with nuance. (That's true even in person, let alone in print communication without body language, facial expression, or tone.) This discussion is primarily for church leaders: clergy, pastoral staff, and those already stewarding their calling and living into a higher level of leadership, accountability, and vocation. Because so many leaders I've coached carry frustration and grief around this subject, I invite you to pause and pray.

God, you see the burdens Your children carry when we are all trying to honor You by living out our faith and calling with integrity. Some of my brothers carry heavy burdens, and I thank You for their commitment to live as men of character. Some of my sisters carry heavy burdens, and I thank You for their commitment to follow Your calling through unseen challenges. Right now, help us to hear each other's concerns, and let us hear Your Holy Spirit as we consider how to steward the calling You've placed on our lives. Sanctify how we relate to each other so that when we pursue Your kingdom, we do no harm as we receive the empowering fullness and confidence of Christ. Amen.

Destructive and Redemptive Disruption: Hurdles, Ineffectiveness, and Truth

Ministerial colleagues—women and men—often find themselves frustrated trying to navigate multiple dynamics and core values as they work together in the church. As a coach, I've heard phrasing like, "to be a responsible husband, father, and pastor, I cannot work that closely with a woman," from my brothers in ministry more times than I can count.

There are many reasons why a church leader might say this. Men in pastoral ministry who find the BGR unhelpful don't want to throw out boundaries altogether, and rightly so. Many are also grieved by scandals involving misuse of clergy power and trust. Those who earnestly pursue personal integrity may value clear, preemptive one-size-fits-all rules in response to the fallout of colleagues' ministry imploding. Others simply need to reframe how they describe attractive colleagues.

(In coaching, I tell men, "Frame what other people will see by how you frame how you see colleagues who are women. Don't refer to her through outward appearance. Begin mentally and verbally describing her as God sees her: as your sister in Christ, a beloved daughter of the King; a co-laborer in the ministry, gifted leader, and anointed speaker and pastor; as someone who strengthens your team because of the spiritual gifts and experience she brings to the table.")

Most pastors know someone who's no longer in pastoral ministry because of a moral meltdown, often involving abuse of power. One church leader said that in almost a decade of denominational leadership, *they didn't deal with a single pastor-to-pastor affair: only pastors with church members or pastors with community members outside the church.* Some pastors have former colleagues who've faced justified prison time. We need to grieve those situations. When ministerial colleagues who are men express hesitancy to reassess the BGR, sometimes it comes from a place of humility, grief, and a deep desire to honor the Gospel of Jesus Christ.

That's not the sole response, though. Some practical feedback I've heard from men I coach include:

- "I had no idea of the scope [of hurdles created by the BGR for pastors who are women]; I had some idea, but I don't know what to do about it."

- For many, the BGR is the only model for sanctified relating that they know.

- Others weren't taught it explicitly, but it was modeled in church cultural expectations.

- Multiple men said they were never given training on how to work with women.

- For those taught to follow Rev. Graham's code, women in the community or congregation weren't differentiated from women colleagues in pastoral leadership or on staff. The takeaway was the same: "never be alone with a woman."

Meanwhile, as my brothers grapple with these concerns, what are some ways the BGR is disruptive for women in church leadership and pastoral ministry?

I first encountered it unexpectedly. God called me to minister as a lead pastor during an ordination class. At the end of "Doctrine of Holiness" with Dr. Chris Bounds, we all held hands to pray. My arms were completely stretched out to those on either side, closing our prayer circle that spanned the room. As I stood there fully surrendering to God, I prayed, "tell me what to do and I'll do it. Anything. Have your way with my life," when I felt a light sensation throughout my whole body. I felt light in spirit and so incredibly loved. Like a download, I *knew* God was inviting me to pursue training to become a lead pastor.

I was terrified. "What if I mess up? I'm lacking *this*, I don't know enough of *that*. Is this even possible?" Then I thought, "at least I'm in a denomination that supports women in ministry, so that's figured out." Finally, I said, "Yes, God; if it's your plan, you will make a way. By faith, I say yes."

My husband and I traveled back home. Later that week, I heard of a posting for a staff position at a church. My husband—my biggest fan and most faithful cheerleader—said, "Get in there! Apply, start asking questions! If you're saying yes to God, you need to start taking steps."

I made an appointment with the senior pastor to discuss the role. As I started asking questions, the pastor said in a matter-of-fact tone, "Katie, I'll stop you right there. I can tell you right now I won't be hiring a woman for this role, because we'll be working too closely together."

I was shocked. I knew there would be hurdles; I was working as a nurse while continuing education, parenting toddlers, and ministering in the local church. But I didn't anticipate that my gender would be my greatest roadblock to following God.

Pragmatically, one place the BGR suffocates leadership growth for women is in small rural churches, which is most churches. Around sixty percent of all churches have one hundred or fewer people in attendance.[4] Sometimes supporters of the BGR assume there are always options or alternatives to meeting one-on-one: "You don't *need* to go out to lunch."

But if you've pastored a small rural church, you know not all congregations have assets others take for granted: full-time secretaries, facilities with heat or air conditioning running on weekdays, or even high-speed internet access. Many churches do not have multiple staff members present in a building at any given time; some congregations rent a building one day a week for worship service only. In rural regions like northern Michigan or Texas, it can take a fire department twenty minutes to get to someone's property; for pastors with tight church budgets, riding in the same vehicle can save hundreds of dollars in gas money.

It's also logistically challenging and unnecessarily burdensome to require a third person to be present for every meeting. Congregations and pastors in those areas matter. On a practical level, the BGR can be further isolating or alienating to rural pastors who are worth the investment of our coaching, mentoring, and collaboration resources.

For women, what is the professional and vocational cost of trying to work with so many hurdles? For many pastors who are women, it can look like this: countless lunches and meetings rescheduled because my spouse could not attend, or a man and I would be alone. It means precious time wasted when all someone wants is to get work done, continue conversations, add glue to professional relationships, and advance the kingdom. If I had to have my husband come with me to all the meetings I need to have with male colleagues, it would be his full-time job.

Sometimes, attempting to follow the BGR "to the letter of the law" led to absurd situations. Often, when I needed to meet with colleagues but there were logistical hurdles because we'd be alone, the solution was returning to our separate offices and meeting over Zoom...alone. Video communication isn't immune to abuse! The solution isn't to pile on more and more bans on specific modes of communication, though. For all pastors, one-size-fits-all rules prohibit forward ministerial movement and productivity.

Dr. Jo Anne Lyon observes, "I have heard of church staff meetings where the men meet separately from the women because they are doing 'a guy thing' and they're 'sure the women wouldn't be comfortable.' What's happening here is the church staff is bonding but the women are left out. These relationships impact decision making, power dynamics, and ultimately the marginalization of women leaders."[5]

"Several years ago, I was at an all-day staff retreat.
It was off-site and my ride left halfway through the day, but
there were plenty of folks I could ride back with. I stayed to
talk to a male co-worker about a work-related matter and
when we were done, everyone had left. I asked him if I could
get a ride back to work with him—and he said no. He got
in his empty car and drove away, leaving me on my own
in an unfamiliar part of town. Perhaps there was a good
reason for him to ride back to work alone... There may be a
specific season when a man needs to keep his distance for a
specific reason. As long as no one is avoiding an entire popu-
lation of people or is roadblocking you from using your gifts,
give him grace and keep doing your thing. But it's another
thing for a spiritual leader, called to shepherd men and
women, to say he wants to avoid an entire subset of people.
This becomes a problem because it assigns ulterior motives
to women whose actual goals are probably quite clear:
I want to serve the church. I want to use my gifts. I want to
work hard. I want to be a part of the team."
— *Dr. Andrea Summers, writing for Missio Alliance* [6]

When God calls you to vocational ministry, God's inviting you to offer your very self: your gifts, time, training, energy, and physical availability. You are led to love, serve, and lead the body of Christ.

When I was told I was ineligible for a ministerial role because I'm a woman, I realized for the first time that while God might name me *called*, others might name me *liability* or *risk* due to something completely out of my control. I knew I was responsible to God for how I responded to the call to ministry and how I carried out the call with integrity. What took time and the wisdom of others to discern was whether I was responsible for my male colleagues' perspectives, or to what degree. Over time, I also discovered how common it is in Wesleyan/holiness denominations for women in church leadership to feel shame (not conviction, but shame), like we've transgressed a line of decency simply by being physically present.

One time a ministerial colleague participated in a discussion panel for a large gathering of pastors. A good-faith, earnest question was asked about the BGR. It can be a difficult topic to bring up; for many, it's the primary model for relational integrity that's been taught. But before the leader addressed the "rule" itself, she named an important dynamic: "just bringing this up has changed the atmosphere in the room for the women here." She was acknowledging that a few words can set loose a wave of humiliating recollections, moments when brothers have named women pastoring in the body of Christ *liability* or *risk* before *sister* or *called*. And no leadership tier is exempt.

In 2008, Dr. Jo Anne Lyon was elected the first female General Superintendent of The Wesleyan Church, a role she carried out alongside two other General Superintendents at the time, Dr. Jerry Pence and Dr. Tom Armiger. All three quickly met, agreeing to travel together and to model how women and men can work together for Christ's church. She notes, "we three worked in this manner together for four years as colleagues serving God and his Church. Not once did I feel minimized or sense any fear among us."[7] However, not all professional colleagues engaged with her in the same way. She continues,

> I remember when we were in a meeting with colleagues from various denominations. Dinner was planned at a restaurant not far from our meeting place. I was not

going to return to the hotel and needed someone to ride with me, so I could find the restaurant. (Full disclosure, I was spending the night with my grandkids.) Around the corner came a respected colleague from another denomination. I bluntly, quickly, and with a laugh, called him by name and said, "Why don't you ride with me to the restaurant so I can find it?" He immediately and in all seriousness said, "I cannot ride with you alone," and moved quickly down the hall. *I still remember the shame that enveloped me in that moment.* A few minutes later, Dr. Armiger came around the corner and, of course, rode with me.[8]

Where one brother responded to her physical presence as a *liability*, another affirmed her identity as *called*. What if knee-jerk reactions to physical presence aren't in alignment with who God shows himself to be and who God shows us we are?

Sisters and brothers, we serve a God who became flesh and blood, who stooped to draw near to us, who even got down on his hands and knees to touch and hold and wash dirty, sweaty human feet. The Word became flesh: and Mary gave birth to him, contractions and umbilical cord and all. Our all-knowing, all-powerful God who sustains the entire universe became incarnate and grew in a woman's uterus. God became human, honoring physical presence and tangible nearness: the Creator of the universe in touchable form, as Philippians 2 reminds us so powerfully.

Proximity isn't the problem, it's the calling.

The problem isn't that we're physical beings: the Word became flesh and was sinless. The problem is that we're fallen, lack healthy boundaries, underestimate ways we abuse power, and fail to see when desire for another human is a signpost to the meaning of ultimate desire, as Augustine expressed: "You have made us for Yourself, and our heart is restless until it rests in Thee."[8]

If proximity isn't the problem, limiting proximity won't ever be a lasting solution. After all, leaders tempted by greed, envy, and power still must find ways to work in proximity with wealth, prestige, and influence.

The solution is to receive the general grace of practical wisdom and insights that equip us to pursue emotionally healthy spirituality, as we also receive the specific grace of Jesus Christ, the Word made flesh who redeems our fallenness but also empowers us with the Holy Spirit. Wherever wooden, one-size-fits-all rules fall short, we find a space where God is calling us to learn as we grow deeper in self-awareness and heart holiness.

And one-size-fits-all rules always fall short.

Regardless of the most noble intentions, practices like the BGR have been found to be largely ineffective.[9] Dr. Lyon notes, "over the years, I have listened to many accounts of male and female pastors who have yielded to temptation. In most cases, *all the rules appeared to be in place,*"[10] while the consistent dynamic was less about sex, more about misuse of power, because affairs were rarely between staff colleagues but frequently between a pastor and employee, church member, or community member. Yet the BGR is still frequently mentioned as the reason women are disqualified from consideration for pastoral roles.

If proximity isn't the problem, limiting proximity won't ever be a lasting solution.

Our moment is similar in some ways to Rev. Graham's but very different in others. There are many ways unhealthy relationships can be carried out; and there are many ways boundaries can be crossed that have nothing to do with physical proximity. When Rev. Graham adopted his shared code, there were no smartphones, one-on-one video calls, or email; there was no instantly accessible internet pornography. Direct-messaging explicit images simply wasn't possible.

Publicly following the "Billy Graham rule" on the surface doesn't automatically mean that we're doing no harm or that we're stewarding our vocation or the vocation of others well. It doesn't automatically mean all is well with our souls, emotionally healthy with our discipleship, or at peace in our habits.

Furthermore, the code Rev. Graham chose to live by also implicitly communicated that he wasn't attracted to men. Then and now, many district leaders and pastors have encountered at least one situation when leaders dutifully following the BGR found it completely irrelevant to same-sex affairs.

Rev. Graham's personal rule was meant to *prevent potential harm* to his remarkable global witness and ministry. The ways it's been adopted and practiced by church leaders who didn't share his circumstances *created a different kind of harm* for women following God's call to pastoral ministry. Some pastors are anxious that without the BGR to follow as a model, all professional boundaries will erode, *potentially leading to further harm.* Meanwhile, wide practice of the BGR *hasn't prevented harm* in the form of clergy misconduct, abuse, cover-ups, and scandal.

> *"In almost all these rules, women are ultimately objectified, and men are seen as weak needing the rules for protection from themselves. Neither person is seen in the strength of God and of whose calling they are following. In general,*

these rules hinder women from providing input into insti-
tutional decision making, developing healthy professional
relationships, learning important information shared in
casual conversation." - Dr. Jo Anne Lyon

The broad application of the "Billy Graham rule" has imposed a high cost for women in pastoral ministry, and without the intended results. Whether you're a pastor, layperson, student, or church leader, many in the church carry all kinds of wounds. Few have been unaffected by local leadership implosion, headline-making scandal, or subsequent cover-ups.

Consider even part of the range of problems among church leaders (heterosexual or same-sex) who followed the "Billy Graham rule":

- Church leader affairs with colleagues

- Abuse of power and misuse of pastoral office: intimate relationships, assault, abuse, or harassment of employees, church members, or community members

- Addiction of both men and women to consumption of explicit online sexual content

- Assault, abuse, or harassment of clergywomen

- Clergy abuse of minors

- Interactions using technology to communicate or share explicit messages or images

- Interactions using technology to share explicit images with minors (a felony)

- Misuse of leadership office: covering misconduct of pastors or church members

Some of the situations listed above are "mandatory reports" in countries like mine: circumstances faith leaders are required to report to law enforcement for the protection of vulnerable children and youth. In the United States, some laws vary state to state, but others are federal.

Sometimes, godly men have paid a high price with their congregations when they've done the right thing and reported misconduct by colleagues or church members. We're never just complying with laws, though; Luke 17:2 makes it clear. We all answer to God.

We also need to wrestle with the fact that for some women who support the BGR, there can be difficult histories and trauma responses associated with being alone in physical proximity with a man. Sometimes assault and rape survivors carry decades-old burdens they've never disclosed to anyone. Sometimes, survivors (women or men) were abused in faith-based settings or by leaders in the church. Every survivor should have the freedom to structure professional interactions in ways that honor their background and allow them to be at ease without having to explain themselves. When one or two trusted colleagues know the "why," they can help navigate practical and social implications.

And sometimes, the gentle grace of God transforms what's labeled a liability—women working on a church staff—into a timely, healing response. In one denomination, a congregation faced a heartbreaking Sunday morning worship service as a regional leader explained the pastor was being removed and provided a brief glimpse into why. (It's never an "affair" when one party is a minor.) During the difficult season of fallout, the interim pastor was a woman with years of ministry experience. Of the challenges she anticipated, she was unprepared for the number of elderly women who quietly sought her out in the weeks and months following. They were the kind of church members who were active volunteers, the heartbeat of a congregation. And they were struggling as the circumstances brought up painful recollections from their own youths that most had never told anyone before. But with a pastor in the pulpit who was a woman, they were finally comfortable enough to share burdens they'd carried alone for decades. When one situation was brought to light in a local congregation, more could come to light, because for the first time, half the church members had a pastor they could feel comfortable with.

Friends, we have the opportunity to work together to hear and honor the truth. Speaking the truth always makes room for more truth to come to light. What seems messy is also the way God brings hope, redemption, and healing.

If we neglect to seek out women to lead on church staff and from the pulpit, there will be brokenness that remains hidden, sometimes carried in isolation for decades by beloved saints of the church. When survivors see someone who looks like them standing in the pulpit (a visible symbol of authority), it can be profoundly powerful and healing. *We need us all together.*

Looking at the church overall, can we take a minute to invite the Holy Spirit into our grief, sorrow, and brokenness?

Visible Rules, Invisible Boundaries: How Men and Women Used to Work Together in the Church

If the BGR is ineffective while also creating hurdles for women to follow their call to ministry, what's the alternative? What can it look like for mentoring to take place without the BGR? Dr. Jo Anne Lyon provides an extremely helpful glimpse into how men in a Wesleyan/holiness denomination invested in her leadership and calling.

One of my first mentors was Dr. O.D. Emery. I was younger then, in my thirties. At that time, he was the President of the Christian Holiness Association. I was the chair of one of the Commissions. Many times, he would pick me up at the airport, drive me to and from the meeting, and talk in his office alone. I asked him many questions regarding how to bring together various groups to a point of action, how one framed questions to lead…Ronald Brannon, [Former General Superintendent] Virgil Mitchell, and Melvin Dieter are some of the men with whom I've had many meetings, eaten in restaurants alone, traveled in their cars alone, talked in their offices with their door closed and without being reminded about its window. I could phone them with questions. They influenced my life at various stages with enormous wisdom and leadership specifics. I learned much about leadership in the church, God's call, conflict resolution, leading large and small meetings, the list goes on. I always felt treated as an equal colleague.[11]

Here, Dr. Lyon is describing her interactions with conservative holiness leaders not that long ago. What a difference in church culture!

How was this possible? She distinguishes between external "visible rules" and practiced "invisible boundaries," saying, "I am grateful for men in The Wesleyan Church who did not know about the visible boundaries and never crossed the invisible boundaries line. They became mentors."[12]

What are the external "visible rules"? These are the explicit, outer practices that have become common over the past few decades among pastors with their colleagues in some church settings (distinct from habits pastors employ when interacting with church or community members). They include:

- Don't ride in a vehicle together
- Don't meet in an office without a window in the door or with the door closed
- Don't talk on the phone unless an assistant is also on the line (or cc'd in email)
- Don't meet one-on-one in public

Yet despite those protocols being enforced—usually quite rigidly—we've seen leaders fall. What were the "invisible boundaries" implicitly practiced by leaders like those who mentored Dr. Lyon? They include:

- *Discussion boundaries*: In professional and mentoring relationships, keeping conversations collegial, not shifting into client-counselor discussions of a personal nature on subjects like personal struggles, marriage, and sex.
- *Self-awareness about power dynamics*: By growing in emotional intelligence and awareness, leaders can be mindful of quiet ways they're tempted to misuse influence and power.
- *Deliberately cultivating work culture*: Strategically planning team activities in ways that do not exclude or minimize the participation of women; practicing transparency.

These "invisible boundaries" structure interactions and relationships in ways that are collegial. Basic professionalism and transparency foster a healthy environment with healthy working relationships. Professional relationships and mentoring dynamics within the church do not then shift toward a counselor-client relationship characterized by discussion of personal matters. The purpose of mentoring, Lyon notes, is to learn professionally from someone more experienced in the profession than the mentee is; it's not a counseling or accountability partner kind of relationship.

These "invisible boundaries" also suggest something else: a simple generosity of spirit toward others that celebrates who they are as humans and who they are in the Body of Christ. These three areas—discussions, self-awareness about power, and creating a welcoming work culture—all form a posture that affirms the personhood of others without identifying them first and foremost as something to consume or resist consuming.

Sometimes, rigid practices around women are described in ways that suggest they're a return to old-fashioned chivalry. But generosity in spirit toward women doesn't have to look like refusing to ride in a car with a woman (and genuine chivalry wouldn't refuse to give a woman a ride). Maybe a more genuine "old-fashioned" generosity of spirit was shown by one of Dr. Lyon's mentors:

> Not once did we talk about our marriages, personal struggles or intimate details of our lives. We always related at a professional, collegial level. I remember a rather humorous time when, at an interdenominational meeting, Dr. [Virgil] Mitchell suggested I attend a specific meeting, saying he would babysit my four children, all under the age of nine. And, he did. He empowered my leadership by giving me voice (which he already had) at this meeting.[13]

What's the outcome of healthy habits that embody invisible boundaries? A professional working relationship empowering us to point people to Jesus.

Professional Communication:
During a hard season, my family received some devastat-
ing news we were grieving. I called a pastor in our local
district office to share the news; our district leaders pray
for each of our pastors. My colleague was compassionate
and professional. In his response, he blended "I" and "we"
language: "Katie, I'm sorry to hear this. My wife and I will
be praying for you, and our district team will be praying
for you." In that exchange, I wasn't seeking comfort from
him personally. I have a counselor and friends for specific
personal support. Talking with my district colleague, I
listed general concerns for which he and district leaders
could pray. Every church leader encounters times they need
a pastor, and I have a few colleagues who pastor me. My
district colleague is one of those people. As a brother and
sister in Christ, our relationship is professionally relational;
we are focused on the mission of the body of Christ,
co-laboring to serve the church.

If we're tempted to worry about what others will think or say, here's what we can pray others see: that men and women can work together in healthy and thriving ways. That they see a glimpse of kingdom fullness and heaven on earth. Jesus listened and obeyed the Father, and within that holiness, he was generous in spirit. Like Jesus, we're called to listen and obey, walking in step with the Holy Spirit.

Snapshot: Healthy Interactions in the Local Church

Rev. Jervie Windom, lead pastor of Resonate Church in Texas, shares practical wisdom about healthy working dynamics from his experience as a military veteran. When a low-ranking soldier meets with a higher-ranking member, they must bring another low-ranking soldier with them or have another senior ranking officer join the meeting. *Higher-ranking officers don't meet alone with a new, low-ranking soldier who is unvetted in character and unproven in battle.*

As soldiers are promoted in rank, they are vetted, seen, known, and tried. They mature, know how things work, and can be trusted to a greater degree. Then, they no longer need to have a third-party present in meetings.

Similarly, when you're discerning how to practice "invisible boundaries" over "visible rules," consider the differences in settings and in your knowledge of people. Ideally, people who have stepped into areas of greater responsibility have been vetted, anointed, and commissioned as their character is refined in ministry. In these circumstances, a baseline of trust can be extended, like higher ranking officers in the military example. There is a difference between trust extended among men and women working together in leadership as ministry colleagues and habits when working with the general congregation, community, and young believers. *"One-size-fits-all" rules like the BGR curb the value of this wisdom because they limit interactions by gender, not by spiritual maturity.*

The leadership at Rev. Windom's church practices "invisible boundaries," not "visible rules." Good fruit is growing from it. Recently he shared, "for the past few years, I have been praying for ministry in greater Houston to open to women. This has been a major prayer point for me. A large church here that is Southern Baptist is now going to support a female church planter and is asking if I would talk to her about our ministry model."

Praise God.

If we see relationships through the lens of God's kingdom, then we can engage with others when we practice discerning what the Holy Spirit is asking for *this* relationship; *this* dynamic; *this* season.

How can we not want to know how God's Spirit wants to bless the kingdom through our relationships with other people? Missing this piece of the value of ongoing discernment misses the whole point. We are called to engage well with others, in community, for the flourishing of the kingdom of God. That is a beautiful vision to live toward with intentionality.

God has placed us in community for a reason. Satan may attempt to twist good things into distorted shadows of the original intent, but community remains a means of grace, despite the ways it can be broken. God has given all of us free will, and we all make choices every day. We know that ever since the birth of the church, until Christ returns, church leaders won't always make good choices, no matter what "visible rules" are in place. But we also know that God wants to sanctify his church and that we've been given the Holy Spirit, who calls, equips, sanctifies, and empowers us to live more and more like Jesus Christ.

Practicing discernment means keeping in step with what the Holy Spirit is asking you to do in specific relationship dynamics. Discernment requires true abiding and listening in the Spirit. It means leaning into the church, accountability partners, spouses, counselors, coaches, and mentors. One of the ways we grow in and through community is through healthy accountability with a trusted accountability partner or discipleship band.

When we practice high expectations and high accountability, we also need to practice high support. This means supporting our pastors and church leaders with time, tools, and relationship-building. Every pastor needs the opportunity to access resources to pursue integrity within relationships of intentional accountability. Whether church leaders have accountability partners or participate in banded-together small groups like "discipleship bands," authentic relationships of openness, trust, and honesty accelerate our growth.

They curb our tendency toward self-deception, reflecting to us the ways that God is working in our lives.

There are many ways we need accountability; after all, multitudes of pastors have inappropriate relationships…with work. Working sixty, seventy, or eighty hours a week, work is placed before close relationships, marriages, or families.

My accountability partner knows the worst of me: my immature thoughts, petty tantrums, the things no one says out loud, I say out loud. Then once it's been said, it's all in the light and can be dealt with for the good before God.

Without the support of healthy relationships and community, pastors and church leaders can find themselves isolated. Isolation is common in ministry, but it fosters depression, loneliness, and discouragement. It also makes space for our hearts and habits to begin sliding unconsciously away from our values. We are made for community, and it hurts when community breaks down. Thankfully, God is in the business of restoring what has been lost. If you're in a place or season of isolation, find at least one safe person to reach out to and connect with.

Where following the law lets us think we can coast on "autopilot," God's Word (Gal. 5:16-25, Eph. 4:16-25) requires more of us. The Gospel of John delivers these words to believers: "be one as I and the Father are one" (John 17:21). God is inviting us to keep in step with the Holy Spirit.

When we approach our calling with awe and a healthy, appropriate amount of "fear and trembling," you and I won't be driven to settle for one man's list of rules. How we steward our calling, integrity, relationships, accountability, and leadership matters so much that it demands much *more* of us than following one man's code of conduct ever could. We'll be driven to do the hard work of ongoing discernment. We'll be driven to do the hard work of maintaining accountability in relationships of trust, maturity, and discretion. We'll be driven to do the hard work of investing in the health of our closest relationships. We'll be driven to question our motives, to be wary of platforms, spotlights, and praise.

And we'll be driven to honor the Body of Christ by holding accountable all who try to wear the church like camouflage as they prey on, abuse, exploit, and diminish those in their care, those who are vulnerable, and those who lack the platform, status, or goodwill to defend themselves against accusations of dishonesty.

First: Do. No. Harm.

It is heartbreaking to see the body of Christ ripped apart, witness tarnished every time a congregation or organization struggles so deeply to name the evil in its midst that it would rather brush over unpleasantness than stand squarely with those who've suffered because of shepherds in wolves' clothing. Jesus was clear: it's better to have a millstone around the neck and be thrown into the sea than to harm or exploit innocent, vulnerable people.

That means part of the hard work of church leadership is accepting the reality that not all who need to leave their pulpits should be reinstated to pastoral ministry or leadership roles. That doesn't diminish God's grace: it strengthens the grace of accountability. It bears witness to the grace of protection for the vulnerable. When ministers who must take leaves of absence are genuinely remorseful, they don't resent the healthy boundaries that reinforce the personhood of all involved. With humility, they accept that through the transforming grace of Jesus Christ, they may receive grace as a church member, even if pastoral ministry is no longer a vocational option.

This also means part of the hard work of the wider church can be to prepare and be ready to "do no harm" by supporting pastoral spouses and families left financially and socially vulnerable in the wake of an exit from ministry. With generosity and kindness, we can serve those who suffer through no fault of their own, bearing witness to the love of God who will never let them down.

What if the *reason* for using the Billy Graham rule and the *fall-out* from deploying it in ways that harm women *both* illustrate the prayer of confession? "We have not loved you with our whole heart; we have not loved our neighbors as ourselves..."

God is calling us to return to our First Love, God himself—to love God with our whole hearts. God is also calling us to love our neighbors as we love ourselves: to approach others in our proximity in ways that aren't directed toward gain, but toward joyful giving. Lust and selfish ambition are the same sin, just pointed at different goals. Both look for what they can gain, possess, consume, and benefit from. Even if it were possible to fast from the presence of whole categories of people, it still wouldn't address the posture of the heart that needs to be transformed by God's sanctifying grace.

We don't just need better boundaries; we need to ask God to do for us that we cannot do for ourselves and sanctify us in perfect love that sweeps away our need to possess, consume, use up, dominate, throw away, and destroy.

The prayer of confession is usually said by a congregation of worshipers. Then, the pastor prays: "Almighty God have mercy on us, forgive us all our sins through our Lord Jesus Christ, strengthen us in all goodness, and by the power of the Holy Spirit keep us in eternal life. Amen."

Strengthen us in all goodness.

What a beautiful vision of the body of Christ working and training together: being strengthened in all goodness. You and I need cardiovascular exercise for a healthy heart and brain. We also need weight training for strong muscles that help keep us balanced, for strong bones that resist breaking.

Strengthen us in all goodness.

When we confess we've failed to love God with our whole selves and failed to love our neighbors selflessly, when we repent and ask forgiveness—

God does for us what we cannot do for ourselves.

Thankfully, the Holy Spirit is eager to shape every "yes" of our hearts into deeper discernment and wisdom. God is calling us to work with the Holy Spirit to be strengthened in all goodness. It takes time, it's not easy, and it can be hard to trust that progress is being made. But God doesn't want to leave us here.

God's not asking me to be Billy Graham. God's not asking you to be, either. God made you *on purpose* and *for a purpose.* Like the shepherd David, I can't move around wearing King Saul's armor; I have different weapons to wield. What are assets for one person aren't automatically gifts for another. David had speed, aim, hours spent on target practice, experience taking down moving targets larger than he was. He needed to be nimble, to judge distance and speed almost instantly, to feel the weight of the stone, to let muscle memory take over. He did not need to be weighed down in someone else's armor like a slow, unresponsive tank.

What if we can live into our purpose and carry out our calling with integrity—without feeling the need to wear someone else's armor?

Come, Holy Spirit, and strengthen us in all goodness.

Chapter Nine Reflection & Discussion Questions

Rev. Dr. Anita Eastlack, Director of Evangelism and Discipleship for the Northeast District of The Wesleyan Church & Lead Pastor of Crosspoint Wesleyan Church, PA

Rev. Lance writes, "In all the conversations I have as a coach, I find men and women are looking for workable models of healthy engagement." As you prepare your heart and mind for reflection, consider Jesus as a model—humble, full of grace, and perfect in all his ways. He had conversations with women, related to women, touched women, and allowed women to touch him. After his resurrection, Jesus was with a woman—alone, in the garden, just the two of them. Consider his pure heart, his pure conversation, his pure example. As you reflect, seek the Jesus way, perhaps with the tune, "Open the eyes of my heart, Lord."

Discussion Questions

1. *This chapter covers...a lot. How are you doing? Need a drink of water? Need to stretch your legs? Few church members, congregational leaders, pastors, or regional leaders have been unscathed by grief or disillusionment because a leader, colleague, or friend has betrayed trust, crossed boundaries, or preyed on someone vulnerable. Are there things you're still grieving?*

2. *Do you believe the Holy Spirit can transform us this deeply?*

3. *If you need to talk with someone, do you have people you can talk to this week?*

4. This chapter includes a list of three helpful invisible boundaries. Take some time to discuss these within your small group in the context of application in your world. Would you and your group add other invisible boundaries to this list?

5. As Wesleyan leaders, we approach this topic from the viewpoint that it is about living a holy life. Read Ephesians 4:29-32, Titus 1:6-9, and Galatians 5:13-26 and discuss what stands out to you in these passages.

This Week

Slow down and ask the Holy Spirit if there's anything you're avoiding. With God's kindness and the gift of trusted others, can you look it in the eye and name it? With the Holy Spirit and others, ask God to make all things new. With support, take a practical, concrete step. Ask God to renew your freedom, peace, and joy.

CHAPTER TEN

Side By Side: Co-Laboring Joyfully in the Fullness of the Holy Spirit

"As iron sharpens iron, so one person sharpens another"
(Prov 27:17).

I pastored a church in a rural, economically depressed community. One day I was driving through a McDonald's parking lot and saw a disgruntled man in the later decades of his life yelling outside. He'd gotten himself kicked out.

It takes a lot to get kicked out of a McDonald's, but this gentleman had just earned a lifetime ban. I asked him how his day was going. It turned out he'd gotten kicked out of Burger King, too.

Some days are like that.

So, I invited him to church.

And he came. Being in a church service was a new experience for him. His presence was a new experience for some of the church members, too. But eventually, he became part of the congregation.

In the congregation, some members couldn't read. About half didn't have access to high-speed internet. One church member in their seventies didn't know how to write their own name–until deciding to learn so they could sign the pastoral Christmas card. As a pastor, few things have moved me as deeply as that did.

In regions like this, adult literacy specialists and other resources are not in abundant supply. How would you carry out discipleship and spiritual formation, if one-third of your congregation was illiterate or read at a third-grade level? How would Sunday morning worship services look if bulletins or slideshows with text were useless to half of the gathered worshipers? If the internet speed is slow, online resources or literacy tools are inaccessible.

The years I spent as a nurse catalyzed my ability to see, name, and accept what's in front of me so that my response is fitting, timely, and maximizes whatever tools I have at hand. As a nurse or as a pastor, part of the job is seeing who is in front of me right now, as they are. Then, I can ask the Holy Spirit to help me know how to respond.

On the day my future church member was banned from McDonald's, this guy had already been a hassle who made employees' hard days harder. For me that day, the Holy Spirit was as persistent as a hospital call button and nudged me to look beyond the exterior. Adult illiteracy is a complex, big-picture challenge, but the Holy Spirit doesn't let me ignore the belligerent guy yelling in my community McDonald's parking lot.

Our congregation had to be practical. For discipleship and spiritual formation, we used very few book-based studies. Outside of Sunday mornings, we found creative ways to engage scripture, like listening to CDs, watching "The Chosen" on DVD, and video series. For Sunday mornings, any projected content (like the slides prepared for sermons) had to be heavily image-based, not text-heavy.

And people who'd never been inside a church building got saved. They started getting sober. Sometimes, it got messy; actually, most of the time. I smile at how the moments when we saw God move most powerfully were also the most chaotic moments as we entered uncharted territory.

How are we affected by the presence of anyone being made new in God's grace? They sanctify us. They reveal what's in our hearts, they sand off the rough edges of our own spirits, they crack open our hearts and help us grow in holy love and humility, and they bring the kingdom of God nearby. They make us better, and they hold us accountable.

How are we affected by the presence of anyone being made new in God's grace? They sanctify us.

Wherever we are in our spiritual growth, we're all still being made new in God's grace and by God's grace. Life in community constantly provides ample space to be shaped into deepening Christlikeness. This has been true from the New Testament early church to Brother Lawrence famously practicing the presence of God in his busy kitchen to early Wesleyan Methodists who met in transformative small accountability groups: sisters and brothers in Christ experience God's sanctifying grace in the context of shared life together.

God has this amazing gift to give us: community, where we are brought into proximity of people who will be an avenue of grace to us—if we allow them to be. That's a 360-degree truth: kingdom fullness jumbles us in together, for our own good, even when it is new or uncomfortable or uncharted territory.

I'm no stranger to the ways community can stretch you and challenge familiar patterns of sharing life and worship—even in ways like how scripture is presented or how the Gospel is visually communicated during Sunday morning worship.

Sometimes it's uncomfortable. I get to know myself in new ways when I discover a new learning curve. It takes grace and humility to grow with good humor; to grow *in* community, *through* community, and *in front of* community.

But if I'm not willing to do that–why am I in ministry? The book of Acts is full of stories of the amazing power of the Holy Spirit, and Acts is also full of stories about uncomfortable growth. They're the same stories.

If I want the power of the Holy Spirit without the awkward discomfort the early church experienced, I'm not living the Gospel of Jesus Christ, I'm living the life of a tourist. But Jesus didn't call me to be a tourist, he called me to tell people about Jesus and to equip and mobilize believers. If it was uncomfortable for Paul and Barnabas and Peter and the others, why would I have it any easier? A kingdom-full community of faith is one where our actions are propelled more by God's love than they are by our desire to avoid potential discomfort.

The Community of the Called: Co-Laboring for the Gospel

When women and men work side by side in God's kingdom, we have the opportunity to ask the Holy Spirit to use those experiences and interactions to make us more like Jesus and to empower us to love as Jesus loved.

The New Testament is crammed with stories of the Holy Spirit anointing early believers to co-labor for the Gospel. Priscilla and Aquila, Timothy, Barnabas, Phoebe, Silas, and many more come in and out of view as we watch the early church in Acts scatter in empowered witness. But very quickly in Acts, we see that empowered witness didn't prevent misunderstanding or conflict. Even in the context of miraculous signs and wonders, perspectives and personalities mingled and clashed. Then and now, working side by side helps us grow in holiness, if we humbly choose to let it.

That was true when Paul and Barnabas had a "sharp dispute" over intern John Mark (Acts 15:36-40, 2 Tim. 4:11). It was true when Paul confronted Peter "to his face" (Gal. 2:11-14). It was true when the Greek-speaking Jewish widows were left out of daily food distribution while the Hebraic Jewish widows continued to receive their meals (Acts 6:1). It was true for Euodia and Syntyche, women in Philippi who contended for the Gospel side by side with Paul. Paul included them with his other co-workers: "I plead with Euodia and I plead with Syntyche to be of the same mind in the Lord. Yes, and I ask you, my true companion, help these women since they have contended at my side in the cause of the gospel, along with Clement and the rest of my co-workers, whose names are in the Book of Life" (Phil. 4:2-3).

If co-laboring in community was a sanctifying experience for these giants in the New Testament, you and I can expect it will be for us as well. Where God breaks through miraculously in signs and wonders and the gifts of the Spirit, we also find God cultivating the fruits of the Spirit in us. Working side by side makes room for us to practice habits that will give the fruits of the Spirit room to grow.

What are some habits that help us welcome the sanctifying grace of life together as we live in kingdom fullness? As I've coached men and women in ministry, I've noticed powerful habits clustered around these practices:

- Prayerfully listening
- Generously empowering
- Pragmatically envisioning

Each of these includes practical habits you and I can practice as we interact together in our work. Like any new habit, these are simple to talk about, but they take time and intentionality to put into place and practice consistently. Like any new habit, *practice* is key. We are all learning and practicing as we go, with room to try and try again. Like any new habit, these practices take persistence around unforeseen hurdles; they take good humor in the face of discouraging naysayers; they take focus when you are tempted to compare yourself to someone else; and they take creativity as you explore what they look like in your life, for you.

Prayerfully Listening

In an earlier chapter, I described the joy I experienced working as a nurse, when I slid on my stethoscope and listened deeply. In medical settings, it's crucial to listen physically to a patient's chest or abdomen. This kind of listening requires both focus and proximity.

As co-laborers for the Gospel, mindful communication with each other is essential. Practicing healthy boundaries with time and our relationship to work can free us to be powerfully present more, distracted less. I can't listen well to your heartbeat through a stethoscope if I'm wearing my instrument in one ear while propping my phone to the other as "hold" music plays. And as a leader, I can't listen to what you're trying to say—or what the Holy Spirit is trying to do through our interaction—if I'm inattentive.

How many misunderstandings result from distracted listening? How much miscommunication happens because we need practice in the habit of being present in an interaction, whether over the phone, through a note, with an email, on a video call, or in person? "Hot takes" are not a fruit of the Spirit, and it's easy to form an opinion, validate a perspective, or shoot off a response before we know the whole picture, intent, or even facts.

We co-labor well in churches or districts, on committees or in communities, when we slow down, check facts, fall quiet, listen attentively, exercise curiosity, and figure out which questions need to be asked. Leadership isn't always loud, and loud isn't always powerful.

In medical settings, it's not just important to listen to a heartbeat, it's crucial to listen carefully to a patient's words: what they're saying, what they're not saying, or what they're sharing in a roundabout way. If you've ever had a doctor get your information wrong or dismiss your symptoms only to discover later something is critically wrong, you know how important it is for physicians to ask the right questions. If your doctor doesn't hear what you're trying to say, they're less likely to order the tests likely to uncover the right diagnosis and treatment. Good physicians are excellent at listening, sorting out the relevant information, and asking perceptive follow-up questions.

Asking questions is an important habit in all our interpersonal interactions as we work side by side. It's an essential part of listening, which means we value the other person or group enough to pay attention, notice our judgments, and withhold making assumptions. If I ask questions, I'm assuming I don't know everything. I'm assuming there may be something I may need to learn. I'm assuming there might be something I haven't thought of or considered. I'm assuming that asking questions and receiving answers allows the Holy Spirit time and space to illuminate a situation.

Asking questions is an important habit in all our interpersonal interactions as we work side by side.

Asking questions is even more essential when navigating unfamiliar territory. Sometimes this happens on a very small, simple scale.

One time I was part of a discussion on women in ministry and "one-size-fits-all" rules like the "Billy Graham rule." As a male participant considered the implications of approaching professional interactions without a one-size-fits-all rule, he asked about the pastoral habit of placing a hand on someone's shoulder to pray for them, if a pastor who is male is praying for a woman.

"Can I put my hand on someone's shoulder?"

It's vital to ask questions, yet I couldn't be the person to answer that question, because he wasn't praying for me. I answered, "Just ask the person you're praying for if it's okay to put your hand on their shoulder." (In fact, in that kind of situation, it's a good question for pastors to ask in general, not just when the pastor is male and praying for a woman. Not everyone welcomes physical contact; many congregations include members who are managing PTSD, or who have autism and may find physical touch distracting or a stressor.)

My response to the pastor empowered him to take that question into his daily interactions. *As we work side by side, one way to demonstrate respect for each other is simply to ask someone if they have a preference, and then practice trying to honor it.*

Asking questions is also an important part of navigating paradigm shifts. Whenever we face institutional/organizational change or a hard topic, asking questions is an essential habit. How I define a challenge is largely shaped by my own known and unknown assumptions. When I ask questions, the answers can puncture my false assumptions or reveal assumptions I didn't know I was making.

When women and men work side by side, there will be plenty of opportunity for accidental miscommunication, genuine conflict, or pot-stirrers to stir up division. Practicing the habit of prayerful listening can defuse problems preemptively. Prayerful listening shapes our posture toward conflict. And it can keep us on our guard against the enemy's attempts to sow discord, distrust, and division.

If we choose to approach interactions with curiosity, we release the burden of feeling like we need to have all the answers. When you practice the habit of listening deeply, you'll find yourself empowered to ask questions that will propel your effectiveness as you discover unexpected responses and new avenues of engagement.

Generously Empowering

Only after listening deeply and responding with curiosity can we move into a shared posture of generously empowering each other. I can't equip someone effectively if I don't know what challenges they are facing. Working side by side means hearing our colleagues and then continuing to communicate with them as together we identify hurdles to kingdom flourishing. This dovetails with stewarding vocation and calling. While stewarding vocation can happen in part at organizational and institutional levels, sometimes at the personal level, it looks like empowering our co-laborers to flourish in kingdom fullness.

When I'm coaching or mentoring someone, as I pray, I ask, "What is their next 'yes' to God?"

It's obvious but worth saying: this means that what we are *not* doing is listening deeply to gain an advantage from the fact a colleague is facing a challenge. Your colleague is more than your colleague, they're your co-laborer in the kingdom, contending with you for the Gospel of Jesus Christ. Your co-laborers are your teammates, not your competitors. Ministry is not a playground game of "king of the hill," everyone scrambling to be on top.

If you allow yourself to become preoccupied with building a platform, you will find it more and more difficult to resist a sharp-edged protective posture toward your self-promotion—and the less you will resemble Jesus Christ. Generously empowering others means that instead, you are looking "not only to your own interests but also the interests of others" (Phil. 2:4).

When I'm coaching or mentoring someone, as I pray, I ask, "What is their next 'yes' to God?" Part of my calling as a leader is to ask where the Holy Spirit might be leading someone as they grow in grace and discover their gifts and vocation in each season. It's beautiful to be part of the process of empowering someone's calling. When you consider opportunities that come your way or options that seem like savvy choices, ask God to show you how to steward those in such a way that others are generously empowered.

What are some practical ways you and I empower others? Sometimes empowering others overlaps with ways to catalyze leaders, like taking someone along to a conference or making space for emerging leaders to interact with established leaders.

Sometimes, empowering others looks like finding space for them to exercise their calling and practice their gifts. If your denomination or organization has empty pulpits and women who are called and trained but can't get local boards to consider them as pastoral candidates, sometimes there's an opportunity for creative ministry impact. In my denomination, for a variety of reasons, sometimes congregations enter what's called "developing church status." When a church is placed in "developing church status," the district can appoint the pastor. It's a wonderful opportunity for our district superintendents to appoint called, equipped, anointed women as interim ministers, providing churches experiences with pastors who are women. This relational proximity provides space for congregations to experience the anointing and giftedness of women in pastoral leadership when they might otherwise resist calling a woman. Frequently, congregations or individual members who had been wary or previously opposed to the idea of a woman leading their church end up becoming some of the strongest and loudest supporters. When a woman is appointed to pastor a congregation in "developing church status," both she and the church are empowered to discover how the kingdom of God is at work in their midst. This is one very practical way district leaders can generously empower both pastors and congregations.

At times, empowering individuals looks like showing them different sketches of daily ministerial life. When I coach or mentor emerging leaders who are women, sometimes I hear questions like, "I think God is calling me to_____ but I don't know if it's possible. I haven't seen that. How would it work?" Frequently I'm asked questions like, "How do you navigate being a mom and pastor or having a family and ministry?" In those moments, I offer my experience, often describing the flexibility of ministry in lead pastoral roles. (In fact, of all my local church roles, I've had the most flexibility as lead pastor.) When I share my experience, I empower emerging leaders by answering their questions, clearing misconceptions, describing pragmatic implications, and encouraging them to begin picturing what pastoral ministry might look like in their lives.

One week, I experienced something unique. I had conversations with four different lead pastors at the same time of day—and we were all sitting and waiting in school pick-up lines. During a couple of calls that were longer conversations, when the kids got in the car, we paused our chats, hung up, took the kids home, got them started on snacks and homework, and then resumed our calls. Like remote employees with flexible scheduling, we were able to creatively adapt our workdays. It's possible to engage meaningfully without sacrificing ministry effectiveness or valuable family interactions.

Women and men both need the freedom to practice healthy work-life habits, and our churches are better for it. Showing up for our spouse, friends, children, or family keeps pastors accountable for delegating, which is something we're not known for being good at. But pastors are called to equip the saints to do the work, and when we practice healthy boundaries and habits and we delegate well, then we can empower staff members and lay members.

When I share that kind of experience with emerging leaders, whoever they are, I'm illustrating one way any pastor responsible for children can engage in ministry and parenting. Offering practical examples clears some of the fog around ministry life (especially for those who didn't grow up in parsonages or who grew up in ministerial families that didn't have healthy habits). By describing how we as leaders intentionally approach vocation, we can clear up uncertainty and model healthy flexibility. Ministry and family are compatible; ministry and friendships are compatible; ministry and meaningful community are compatible.

Jesus didn't stay awake working 24/7 during his three years of public ministry. He slept, went to weddings, visited friends, withdrew to pray. Leading and co-laboring with transparency invites others to picture themselves living into their next "yes" to God as they shift from hesitating with uncertainty to imagining with hope.

The Holy Spirit places us in community; that is intended to be an anointed gift. When you first say "yes" to God, it's not always obvious that your "yes" or my "yes" can help someone later find their own "yes" to God's calling. As an unmarried man, the Apostle Paul wrote a large chunk of the New Testament and co-labored alongside many other believers, traveling with married couple Priscilla and Aquila, mentoring young Timothy, and allowing the church at Philippi to embrace him like family. Joanna, a disciple of Jesus who traveled with him, was married. Her husband was Chuza, who worked for Herod in a high-ranking job; as a woman of means, she was a significant financial supporter of Jesus' public ministry (Luke 8:3; 24:10). Lydia, a luxury retailer, responded to God as she listened to Paul's message; she led her household in being baptized, and a few verses later, we find that her house is already a hub for believers (Acts 16:11-40).

Your "yes" to God will empower others to begin picturing and imagining their "yes" to God in ways you can't always see yet. When you contend for the Gospel of Jesus Christ, you're not only handling your individual calling. You are standing in the light, opening the door for others to come with you or placing them on your shoulders so they can reach further than you can.

Your goal is to have others around you accelerate to their capacity, and at best, it's greater than yours. This is part of why the enemy tries to discourage, distract, or divide you from your calling: because it's never just *your* calling. Your "yes" can empower someone else to see their "yes." The Holy Spirit can reach people through you that I can't reach. The Holy Spirit can reach people through me that you can't reach.

This is life as the body of Christ: many members, one body, anointed and empowered by the Holy Spirit to proclaim the good news of Jesus Christ, to carry the light that the darkness cannot overcome, to announce the inbreaking kingdom of God that the gates of hell cannot prevail against. When "God-fearing Jews from every nation under heaven" were staying in Jerusalem and heard the sound of the Pentecost wind and each heard the words being spoken in their own language, a witness was planted in each of those languages: "we hear them declaring the wonders of God in our own tongues!" (Acts 2:1-12). Jesus Christ stands at the door and knocks, calling all people to himself, inviting us to take part together in the life of his body.

God is calling us to witness the light of the world, Jesus Christ, co-laboring side by side. Christ is calling unmarried people and married people, non-English speakers and English speakers, people with health and people with disabilities, people with wealth and people without, literate people and people who are illiterate, neurodivergent people and neurotypical people, people of every race and ethnicity, aging people and young people, people who work and witness in the marketplace and people called to full-time ministry, incarcerated people and free people: we are called and equipped and empowered, side by side, united in Jesus Christ, through Jesus Christ, for Jesus Christ, in the power of his name and to the glory of God.

When we hear the "wonders of God" declared in the languages and words and lives of brothers and sisters who are different from us but united with us through Christ Jesus, we are set free to empower each other with radical generosity.

When we hear the "wonders of God" declared in the languages and words and lives of brothers and sisters who are different from us but united with us through Christ Jesus, we are set free to empower each other with radical generosity. Responding to the wonders of God at work in others' lives always demands our utmost. As we share life in community, the habits we pursue will both reflect and shape our values.

Pragmatically Envisioning

Emerging leaders benefit as individuals when they're able to shift from vague uncertainty to concrete examples of life in ministry. Similarly, as co-laborers in the kingdom practice generously empowering each other, there's another valuable habit that involves practical vision. Practicing pragmatic vision is one way we welcome the sanctifying grace of life together. Like the other habits, it takes intentionality. What do I mean by practical or pragmatic envisioning?

I mean goals with shoes on.

I mean vision with a roadmap.

It's easy to make New Year's resolutions; it's hard to go to the gym when it's thirty degrees and already dark at four in the afternoon. To achieve my resolutions, I don't just need a goal of exercising or going to a gym three times a week. I need a plan for identifying and working around big and small hurdles that make it easy to stay home and hard to get out the door.

Sometimes pragmatic envisioning is practiced as an individual habit; sometimes it's pursued in a team setting when differing co-laborers bring gifts to the table that complement each other. Either way, pragmatic vision becomes urgent when we pursue it as part of our work in generously empowering others to follow God's call.

One time I was in a setting where a lofty goal was championed: leaders were praying to see the number of women in lead ministry reflect the general population. That would mean fifty percent of lead pastors in that context would be women. It was a fantastic goal bursting with kingdom fullness and would require the work of God to be lived out.

The challenge was this: *how* was it going to happen? At the ground level, the ingrained culture and processes underlined that the goal was a beautiful vision honoring God, but to be attainable, the established practices and habits in place would somehow have to change in pragmatic ways. There weren't pipelines for recruiting women consistently through different leadership roles; there wasn't consistent willingness from pastors who were men to work with pastors who were women. An audacious vision was championed; the question was how it would come to fruition without processes and pipelines in place to empower women and men alike to say yes to God's calling.

In that context, there was a holy vision—*high expectation*—alongside an absence of habits, tools, and processes to pair this God-sized vision with *high accountability* and *high equipping*. The value expressed in the vision was specific: we value women responding to God's call to ministry in lead pastor roles because God doesn't call women as an exception to the rule, God calls women into ministry as a regular feature of kingdom fullness. The vision was also specific: we are praying for God to call and raise up women for pastoral ministry, we want to see this, and we dream of living into kingdom fullness to the degree that at least half our lead clergy members are women. The vision was specific, and it reflected specific values from leadership. The vision just needed processes to facilitate it into concrete tools and actions. It also needed accountability mechanisms to call male co-laborers to explicitly commit to our Wesleyan Methodist holiness heritage that celebrates women in all ministry roles.

The Holy Spirit is always at work in both the vision and the plumbing, so to speak. For every goal or dream, someone is renting a venue, checking local permits, washing guest sheets, corralling extension cords, or fixing the Wi-Fi. It's not always possible for one leader to both *envision* and *envision pragmatically*; sometimes, our gifts are for one or the other.

Thankfully, God puts us in community for just that kind of reason. When the Hellenistic widows were left out of food distribution, the apostles could have responded with a vision statement in support of consistent or expanded food ministry; but they initiated a prayerful, pragmatic response proportionate to the need from an existing pool of leaders who were identified as gifted and willing to respond to the dynamics of the cross-cultural situation. When God moves, we need witnesses and leaders who articulate the vision, and we need witnesses and leaders who steward the vision pragmatically. Sometimes that's the same person; sometimes, it takes a team.

Grace in the Outpouring, Grace in the Port-a-Potties

In the winter of 2023, a remarkable outpouring of the Holy Spirit flooded Hughes Auditorium on the Asbury University campus in Wilmore, Kentucky. It wasn't the result of a leader's vision, though some people had been laboring in prayer for several years beforehand. This outpouring, an unforeseen move of God,[1] didn't result from any human strategy or planning. No one could have orchestrated or engineered what unfolded over several weeks in a tiny Kentucky town that overflowed with global visitors and traffic jams to the point that the police department eventually had to close the town temporarily. University administrators, ground crews, professors, students, and janitors all scrambled to accommodate what was happening.[2] At first, students came and went as a chapel service extended into ongoing hours of prayer, worship, confession, and testimony. Then vanloads of students from other colleges started coming. Gradually more visitors began to arrive, and people who remembered the famous Asbury revival in the 1970s took notice. Word continued to spread, and then lines of people began forming as they waited in the cold and rain to enter the auditorium where student-led prayer and worship continued. As the outpouring gained more and more attention, visitors started coming from farther away. The seminary across the street and local United Methodist and Baptist churches opened their doors as additional closed-circuit telecast overflow sites. Lines for Hughes Auditorium were hours long, and college and seminary students and professors struggled to find parking as classes continued.

My country has experienced sharp divisions; but a friend who went to Wilmore at the height of the crowds saw tattooed Southern "good ol' boys" next to immigrants and international visitors speaking different languages and wearing face masks, while in one seminary overflow chapel lobby, a bottle of chewing tobacco spit sat on a table. A diverse crowd waited patiently, including elderly people with walkers, families with sleeping babies, Christian celebrities, Appalachian visitors, Catholics, Protestants, retired professors, and visitors from halfway around the world. No focus group, algorithm, or demographic researcher could have predicted (or would have recommended) putting all these people together for hours in long lines.

Later, law enforcement reported that despite tens of thousands of unexpected visitors, despite fringe street preachers showing up with bullhorns, not a single fight broke out, and not a single arrest was made. Worshippers in Hughes representing a variety of denominations reported extraordinary encounters with the supernatural presence of God as a sense of timelessness inundated them in a deep experience of God's love; others reported direct, divine, supernatural healing.

In the midst of all that, students led all the worship; professors volunteered to push wheelchairs of elderly visitors; janitors stocked and restocked toilet paper and kept toilets unclogged; ground crews set up portable shelters to provide cover for those waiting in line in cold rain; port-a-potties sprouted up in rows; stacks of pizza appeared as people from other states sent food to behind-the-scenes volunteers; residents hosted strangers with nowhere to sleep; law enforcement directed traffic; a local church shared its buses, shuttling visitors back and forth when parking was moved to the edge of town; an out-of-state Chick-fil-A employee coordinated efficient line management; volunteers answered constantly ringing phones; security was put in place; the Salvation Army distributed hot coffee to people waiting in the cold; seminary students ushered visitors in overflow sites; a blend of volunteers moved in and out of altar prayer teams in Hughes.

All this, spur of the moment; all this, side by side for the kingdom.

There is grace in the outpouring. And there is grace in the port-a-potties. The Holy Spirit is at work in the vision and at work in the logistics that sustain God's movement.

When the Holy Spirit gives us a holy vision for kingdom fullness, we have the opportunity to embrace and pursue a big-picture vision that communicates high expectations (established and maintained by leaders in positions of authority and those on boards). With that audacious envisioning that champions kingdom fullness, we also practice the habit of implementing vision with humble, practical application. This happens when we pair robust vision with high ongoing accountability and high support, equipping and empowering everyone involved in the process.

Pragmatic envisioning creates space to respond to the movements of the Holy Spirit with a clear vision. It's a habit that creates space for us to welcome the sanctifying grace in our shared life together. It receives a vision of the kingdom and then keeps the parking lot plowed, implements a process to accommodate crowds, hunts down extra trash cans, and notices when they're full. Pragmatic envisioning empowers us to respond to God with equipped readiness. It empowers us to empower each other forward into kingdom fullness.

As we practice habits related to deep listening, generous empowering, and pragmatic envisioning, we welcome the Holy

Spirit to anoint our interactions and work so that life together becomes an avenue of our sanctification.

Come, Holy Spirit! Help us to identify and practice habits in community that will welcome Your inbreaking kingdom in hopeful, practical ways. Thank You for the gift of community that sharpens us and gives us opportunities to grow more like You.

Chapter Ten Reflection & Discussion Questions

By Pastor Randy Lance, Co-Planter and Executive Pastor, Thrive Church, MI

In the kingdom of God, women and men partnering to work side by side can reflect the fullness of Christ's love and mission. When we co-labor for the Gospel, we open ourselves to the transformative work of the Holy Spirit. God uses our interactions and shared experiences to shape us into the image of Jesus.

This concept is not new; the New Testament is rich with stories of believers—men and women alike—working together to advance the kingdom. Names like Priscilla, Aquila, Timothy, Barnabas, Phoebe, and Silas remind us of the early church's dynamic, diverse community of co-laborers. Despite the miraculous signs and wonders that accompanied their work, these early believers also faced misunderstandings, conflicts, and challenges in their mission. These difficulties did not deter them; instead, they served as opportunities for growth in holiness and unity. Good!

The early church's experiences teach us that working together in God's mission is not always "smooth sailing." Disagreements and conflicts are inevitable, even among those who are anointed by the Holy Spirit. Paul and Barnabas had a sharp dispute over John Mark, which led to their separation in ministry for a time. Paul also confronted Peter publicly when he noticed hypocrisy in Peter's actions. These examples demonstrate that conflict is a natural part of co-laboring for the Gospel, but it also presents an opportunity for sanctification if we approach it with humility and a desire to grow in Christlikeness.

With so much information available to us today, sometimes it's easy to forget there have been many times in history that humble us,

God-fearing people have fought for those that are the least of us, the unseen and unwelcome. My great hope is that we are defined by our desire to be sanctified in the full image of Christ and not by who is allowed or not allowed to represent Hope to the world.

Today, as we explore how to work together in our ministries and communities, we too are invited into this process of sanctification through our shared labor. The Holy Spirit continues to work in and through us, cultivating the fruits of the Spirit—love, joy, peace, patience, kindness, goodness, faithfulness, gentleness, and self-control—as we navigate the complexities of working alongside others.

To thrive in this calling, it's vital to cultivate specific habits that help us live out the fullness of God's kingdom in our daily interactions. As you open yourself to the sanctifying grace of God, allowing him to shape you into a community that reflects his love, unity, and power in the world, how can you prayerfully embrace the habits outlined in this chapter so they become a natural, embedded part of your life?

Discussion Questions

1. *There is a transformative power of community in spiritual growth, even when it's uncomfortable. Can you share a time when being in a faith community challenged you? How did that shape your experience of God's grace?*

2. *Reflecting on the early church's experience of co-laboring for the Gospel, how do you handle misunderstandings or conflicts that arise in the ministry of the church? How can these challenges be seen as opportunities for spiritual growth?*

3. *In what ways can we cultivate the habit of prayerfully listening within our ministry teams? How can this practice impact our communication and collaboration with one another?*

4. *If you're a ministry leader, how do you model healthy boundaries for your congregation and ministry team? What strategies have been effective for you in maintaining this balance?*

5. *How does the concept of generously empowering others align with the idea of stewarding vocations within the church? Have you experienced empowering someone in their calling? How can you support someone who may look, sound, or serve differently than you do?*

6. *As leaders who co-labor for the Gospel, how do we ensure our ministry space reflects the diversity of the body of Christ? What steps can we take to create spaces where voices contribute meaningfully and are celebrated and amplified?*

This Week

Think of someone you know who may be facing some kind of challenge. Is there one way you can listen to, celebrate, or champion them this week?

CHAPTER ELEVEN

Trust: How to Enter Hard Conversations and Listen for the Holy Spirit

Jesus knew that the Father had put all things under his
power and that he had come from God and was returning to
God; so, he got up from the meal, took off his outer clothing,
and wrapped a towel around his waist. After that, he poured
water into a basin and began to wash his disciples' feet, drying
them with the towel that was wrapped around him. When
he had finished washing their feet, he put on his clothes and
returned to his place. "Do you understand what I have done for
you?" he asked them. "You call me 'Teacher' and 'Lord,' and
rightly so, for that is what I am. Now that I, your Lord and
Teacher, have washed your feet, you also should wash one
another's feet. I have set you an example that you should do as
I have done for you. Very truly I tell you, no servant is greater
than his master, nor is a messenger greater than the one who
sent him. A new command I give you: Love one another. As I
have loved you, so you must love one another. By this everyone
will know that you are my disciples, if you love one another"
(John 13:3-5, 12-16, 34-35).

God is within her; she will not fall. Do you recall those words from Psalm 46:5 that I shared early on? These words aren't just for me; they are for the church, the body of Christ. *God is within her; she will not fall.* Resting in that truth sets us free to engage in hard conversations because we are submitting our relationships, interactions, communications—all our shared common life—into God's hands. No congregation or denomination can ever solely belong to us. As Christians, we belong to the body of Christ; the body of Christ doesn't belong to us.

When I pray every morning for the sanctification of God's church, I'm not praying that God will spare us from challenging interactions, as much as I want to avoid them sometimes. The church has never been spared difficult conversations. When I pray for the sanctification of God's church, I'm asking God to make us (all together) more like Jesus as the body of Christ, not just as individuals. I'm asking God to transform us through those very conversations. I'm asking God what his purpose is for our relationships. I'm asking God to empower our witness to others, not through a lack of hard conversations, but through our love for each other in the midst of them.

When I pray every morning for the sanctification of God's church, I'm not praying that God will spare us from challenging interactions, as much as I want to avoid them sometimes. I'm asking God to make us – together – more like Jesus as the body of Christ, not just as individuals. I'm asking God to transform us through those very conversations. I'm asking God what his purpose is for our relationships.

The night that Jesus washed his disciples' feet, he had heart-breaking conversations with the disciples, including Judas and Simon Peter. Judas betrayed Jesus with clean feet. Simon Peter denied knowing Jesus with clean feet. Knowing what would happen didn't make it easier for Jesus, who was "troubled in spirit" (John 13:21). When hard conversations are necessary, Jesus leads the way for us. "No messenger is greater than the one who sent him. As I have loved you, so you must love one another" (John 13:16, 35).

God is within her; she will not fall. If we truly believe it, we're free to approach hard conversations with two vital postures:

- Reverence: *God* is within the body of Christ. The Holy Spirit hovers in the space of relationships, eager to shape them through God's holy, self-giving love. However fractured organizations, relationships, or people may be, God calls the body of Christ to integrity, health, and wholeness. It was Jesus who said, "By this everyone will know you are my disciples: if you love one another" (John 13:35).

- Confidence: *she will not fall.* The body of Christ is robust, enlivened by the very Spirit of God. Sometimes we treat the body of Christ like it's fragile; we may fear that hard conversations will break her. But what we do not own, we cannot destroy. In fact, when we engage in hard conversations with prayer, godly counsel, reverence, and love, our churches, organizations, and denominations can grow in strength, maturity, and Christlikeness. This is part of how we receive God's sanctifying grace.

With Jesus leading the way as our example, strength, and hope, you and I can find the grit to persevere. As Rev. Dr. Anita Eastlack puts it, "don't be afraid of the 'sting' of hard conversations." As Paul wrote in Romans 8:31, "if God is for us, who can be against us?"

God isn't only "for" you or "for" me, God is *for us together*, the body of Christ. Whether the sting of a hard conversation hits you or me or both of us, the Holy Spirit "helps us in our weakness," interceding for us when we don't know how to pray (Rom. 8:26). When the sting in a difficult interaction is felt by someone else, Christ is our model, calling us to graciousness. In vulnerable moments, there may be opportunity to lead others out of the sting—not into condemnation, humiliation, or fear. Together, we can refocus on how to make the sting productive: "let's get to work." In these moments, we're inviting the Holy Spirit to unite us as co-laborers.

God is within her; she will not fall. Ultimately, it is the Holy Spirit calling us to name the breakdowns in how we relate and to renew respect and develop trust. Ultimately, we are all trusting God to sustain the body of Christ and to empower us to live anointed, together.

In this chapter, I'll describe:

- Examples of invisible baggage that can inhibit trust
- Habits and postures essential for fruitfully engaging in hard conversations
- Coaching I share with church leaders in training settings

What We Carry: Invisible Burdens Carried by Leaders Who Are Women

Across hundreds of interviews and training settings, similar comments emerge. Frequently, I hear from church leaders grappling with the baggage of difficult interactions. For some church leaders who are women, it can take years to process the cumulative impact of these repeated negative experiences. The toll is often right under the surface; sometimes it shows up in default expectations for interactions, and other times it extends to challenging someone's perception of their very calling.

In coaching, leaders share very personal frustrations. It's important to name what we carry with us, because we don't always see what our sisters and brothers are bringing with them into routine interactions, much less hard conversations. By naming burdens that are often invisible, we create space for compassion, empathy, and understanding. Added clarity reduces "guessing" about what others are thinking or feeling. These insights can help us approach future interactions with renewed intentionality, patience, and understanding.

Not all traditions or denominations share the same challenges, so church leaders from some settings often carry different baggage. Many of the pastors (both men and women) I coach belong to Wesleyan/holiness denominations, including Assemblies of God, Church of God (Anderson), the Church of the Nazarene, The Wesleyan Church, the Free Methodist Church, and the United Methodist Church.

First, let's look at some of the common invisible burdens carried by pastors who are women as they navigate daily interactions. These occur in addition to ordinary ministry struggles; they specifically relate to the toll of repeated interactions shaped by opposition to women pursuing God's call to ministry. In describing the burdens carried by both women and men, it's an act of good faith to share these vulnerabilities. Some invisible burdens carried by pastors who are women include:

- Hopelessness
- Lack of examples or role models; personal or vocational isolation
- Being labeled, called names, and dismissed as belonging to a negative stereotype

- Internalizing concerns from leaders about the compatibility of pastoral ministry and domestic life
- Lack of confidence or "imposter syndrome"
- Trauma (including hypervigilance, over-explanation, or fight/flight/freeze/fawn response)
- Unforgiveness

That's a lot to unpack – enough to fuel a long discussion in any training setting. First, let's pause. Whether you're interacting with this chapter on your own or as part of a study, slowly revisit each burden on the list, receiving each as a way to pray for church leaders who are women. Invisible burdens are invitations to intercede.

If women in pastoral leadership don't feel comfortable sharing these parts of their experience with you, they may still be gauging whether trust is established. Sometimes they're tired of encountering polite skepticism from men who haven't seen that side of their male colleagues. Sometimes, leaders who are women have learned that some male colleagues encourage women publicly or in one setting but are unwilling to speak up in other settings when women are criticized or spoken about unprofessionally.

Responding to Burdens Carried by Women

If you're a church leader, I invite you to think back over your interactions over the years. Reconsider them through the lenses of some of these "invisible burdens." As you do so, notice your response. If there's discomfort, ask the Holy Spirit to give it a clearer name: maybe it's grief. Maybe it's defensiveness or surprise. Maybe it's anger or remorse. Maybe it's overwhelm or recognition.

Many church leaders (both men and women) share experiences of isolation, lack of confidence, being dismissed as a clergy stereotype, or ministry-related trauma. Women may carry these invisible burdens as a direct consequence of simply being a church leader who's a woman, but you don't have to be a woman to know what it's like to go through a "dark night of the soul" or to experience church trauma.

Pastors who have gone through difficult seasons in ministry have a built-in path toward compassion for any other pastor who's endured difficulty in pastoral ministry. The challenge is establishing some basis of minimal trust so that we can share simply and honestly, grieving for each other, praying for each, and speaking life to each other.

You don't even have to be sure what you think of women in positions of church leadership. If you've ever been "chewed up and spit out" by a toxic congregation, you already know you wouldn't wish that on anyone. As Paul wrote, "Carry each other's burdens, and in this way, you will fulfill the law of Christ" (Gal. 6:2).

There are ways to carry each other's burdens and begin building trust *before* you ever engage in a hard conversation. One of those was already mentioned: regular intercession. There are others as well. Brothers, you don't have to know how it feels to have your call questioned repeatedly or fumble with where to clip the mic box while wearing a dress. What you can do is decide your posture, describe your posture, and practice following through like an offensive lineman in American football: there are times to pray and times to answer your own prayer and practice being the center or right guard (offensive positions that protect the quarterback).

- Decide your posture: From a place of surrender, ask the Holy Spirit how to receive invisible burdens carried by co-laborers who are women. Ask God to clarify what isn't in your control and what is. Of the burdens you do have the ability to influence, ask God to place one or two specific things on your heart to carry consistently in intercession and in practice. If there's something you need to make right, do it.

- Describe your posture: From a place of simplicity, when appropriate, practice proactively verbalizing your posture to your co-laborers who are women. It may be brief; something like, "I don't want to miss the opportunity to share a word of encouragement. (That cues them to what kind of comment is coming.) I don't know the extra burdens you've carried as a leader and pastor who's a woman, but I know it's probably cost you in ways I can't picture. I've been praying/my team has been praying specifically for our colleagues who are women. I may not always get it right and I know building trust takes time and follow-through, I just wanted to say I'm glad we're on the same team." Expect that you may see a variety of reactions: the reaction isn't your responsibility, and there may be an initial reaction and a later response. Some leaders may say thank you; others may seem wary, like they're waiting for the "other shoe to drop" (but you're unsurprised and don't take it personally, knowing some pastors are quietly managing their adrenaline surge as they realize there's no hidden critique coming). Some may find tears welling up. Others may be polite but reserved, waiting to see consistent follow-through.

- Practice following through. Building trust takes time, prayer, and intentionality. Notice who's missing from rooms, publications, committees, and platforms. Occasionally let colleagues know when you've been praying for them (that's a sound practice any time). In the context of your current position, ask your co-laborers who are women if there are hurdles they're facing that you might be able to help tackle. Count the cost ahead of time: protecting a quarterback means taking hits. If the hurdles they face genuinely aren't something in your scope of influence, commit to ready intercession that's poised to advocate.

Notice you can start acting on the first two responses almost immediately. You can write a list and begin interceding today; you can develop and describe your posture over weeks. You can work to follow through and build trust over the coming months and years. It's in your power to relieve some of the invisible burden of hopelessness in a fairly short time.

It's hard to feel hopeless when you know you have a left guard, right guard, and center partnering with you. Offensive linemen don't have to execute perfectly to build lasting trust. Strong teamwork involves ongoing communication, knowing your teammates, integrating feedback, anticipating hits, and keeping the big picture in view.

I can testify personally to the difference this makes. I "go with the goers": when I'm in a challenging setting, if there are a couple of people who are encouraging me and *for me* in that space, then I know I'll find kindness in their eyes. Something as simple as spotting their faces and seeing the safety there helps me brush off rudeness, hostility, and exclusion.

That kind of encouragement can be life-giving. Sometimes in church life, we hear statements like, "if God calls you, there's a place for you" or, "if God's really calling you, he'll make a way." What are women supposed to make of statements like these? It's discouraging to hear that kind of sentiment when congregations refuse the values of their denominations and won't consider résumés from women.

Many women who hear sentiments like these may experience several of those "invisible burdens" listed above; there's nothing like a no-win situation to make you feel hopeless. For some women, the solution is to switch denominations, forge their own paths, or find adjacent ways to participate in ministry. But when co-laborers who are men help shoulder invisible burdens, trust that's been sapped away slowly begins to return, grow, and bear fruit.

What We Carry: Invisible Burdens Carried by Leaders who are Men

When I interview, coach, or train church leaders who are men, the fact they're willing to interact with a pastor who's a woman means they are demonstrating at least a basic level of openness. That's not the case in every context where women leaders engage with ministerial colleagues. In community ministerial associations or similar settings, women may encounter clergy members of other denominations who are actively hostile and opposed to our presence or participation.

In this section, though, I'm describing common burdens carried by church leaders who are men and who are willing to interact with me and willing to receive ministerial coaching from a woman. These brothers also typically belong to denominations like the ones listed earlier. Like the struggles described by women in church leadership, these burdens go beyond regular ministerial challenges; they specifically relate to co-laboring with church leaders who are women.

After intentionally spending hundreds of hours listening to my brothers in Christ in conversation and in coaching, some of the common invisible burdens they tell me they are carrying:

- Uncertainty or skepticism about the biblical and theological foundations of women in all roles and expressions of church leadership
- Uncertainty at multiple organizational levels about how to articulate their support of women in pastoral leadership
- Dread of being "canceled" or labeled sexist or misogynistic for acknowledging uncertainty or attempting to ask good-faith questions, in good faith
- Fear of being "canceled" or labeled "soft" or "liberal" for championing pastors who are women
- Lack of role models and examples
- Concern that the topic is too controversial or not compelling enough to justify spending energy or influence on it, on top of regular ministry demands
- Worry about "worst-case scenarios": "what if I work with colleagues who are women without a 'Billy Graham rule' and then get falsely accused of something?"
- Grief at the fallout of friends' and colleagues' ministerial implosions, creating hesitancy about how to communicate professionally with pastors who are women
- Curiosity about the hurdles women experience and uncertainty about how to be supportive: "I don't know what I don't know—but I want to know"
- Conviction to explore their next "yes" to God as they shoulder the burden of partnering together and learn how to advance kingdom fullness in practical ways

These burdens regularly emerge in settings where I'm coaching pastors or leading training, and it's encouraging to encounter honesty, openness, courage, and curiosity about these questions and concerns. There's also enough here to fuel a long discussion in any training setting, so again, let's pause. I invite you to slowly revisit each burden on this list as well, receiving each as a way to pray for church leaders who are men. Invisible burdens are invitations to intercede.

I am deeply grateful for the men who have taken the time and trusted me with their stories and questions. I was changed by this process as well; it was a sanctifying experience. It made me a better team member, a better advocate for kingdom fullness, a better sister in Christ, a better leader, and a better teacher and disciple-maker.

Again, let's pause. Slowly revisit each concern on this list, recalling that invisible burdens are invitations to intercede. Do any of these burdens surprise, dismay, or encourage you?

Responding to Burdens Carried by Men

Once more, if you're a pastor or church leader, I invite you to think back on your interactions over the years. Reconsider them through the lens of some of the invisible burdens carried by pastors who are men. As you do so, notice your response. If there's discomfort, ask the Holy Spirit to give it a clearer name: maybe it's a surprise. Maybe it's defensiveness or frustration. Maybe it's remorse or overwhelm. Maybe it's recognition.

Some of these burdens grow from a combination of uncertainty, worry, and confusion; some arise to avoid being targeted by online trolls or labeled by colleagues. Yet some of these burdens are also positive burdens: burdens of compassion and conviction for sisters co-laboring for the Gospel.

Sisters, as we intercede over the invisible burdens carried by church leaders who are men, we also can decide our posture, describe our posture, and then practice following through, before we engage in hard conversations.

- Decide your posture: From a place of surrender, ask the Holy Spirit how to receive the invisible burdens carried by co-laborers who are men. Ask God to show you places in your spirit where you've put up with too much, taken responsibility for what wasn't your fault, or minimized ways you've been wronged. Ask God to show you places in your spirit that are closed. From the places that are whole and healthy, ask God for one prayer to carry in your heart for your brothers. If there's something you need to release, forgive, or make right, do it.

- Describe your posture: From a place of simplicity, when appropriate, practice proactively verbalizing your posture to your co-laborers who are men and who are trying to champion their sisters. It may be something like, "I don't want to miss the opportunity to share a word of encouragement. (That cues them to what kind of comment is coming.) I don't know what your ministry experience has been like, but I see your effort and posture toward your colleagues who are women and it makes a difference. Every time you champion your sisters, especially when we're not in the room or part of the conversation, you're shouldering part of the burden we carry. I may not say thank you every time, and I know it takes a lot of leaders working together to bring change. I just wanted to say I'm glad we're on the same team. Your effort and courage aren't wasted." You may see a variety of reactions: again, the reaction isn't your responsibility, and there may be an initial reaction and a later response. Some leaders may say thank you; others may seem wary.

And in this case as well, some may be surprised to find tears welling up.

- Practice following through. Building trust takes time, prayer, and intentionality. Occasionally let colleagues know when you've been praying for them and their families. Continue to verbalize your appreciation to co-laborers who champion leaders who are women; acknowledge the unseen cost of their effort. Celebrate their ministry wins in good faith, and continue to extend goodwill toward those who follow through on tackling obstacles or taking hits.

When we carry each other's burdens, ministry is lighter for us all. Earlier I mentioned that pastors who've gone through hard ministry situations have a built-in path toward compassion. It takes the work of the Holy Spirit and health grown from godly support and counsel. By God's grace, if you see a brother who's given you a hard time enduring a hard ministry season of his own, ask God to let your wounds guide you to compassion for his. We all get our feet washed by Jesus.

Habits that Shape Hard Conversations

Just naming some of the invisible burdens we carry into interactions can give helpful clarity and self-awareness. Many pastors already know this from practicing pastoral care in our congregations: we enter interactions with others differently if we know they're grieving; if they just endured a painful loss or if we learn of some other significant burden they've been carrying. When you know someone is grieving a loss, you're less likely to take something personally, more likely to extend grace; less likely to react with impatience, more likely to quietly help in ways they may not even realize in the fog of grief or shock. When you know a veteran has PTSD, you understand if they quietly slip out of crowded, noisy rooms early. When you know someone just received an earth-shattering diagnosis affecting mobility, you may quietly open a door, slow your walk, wash their coffee cup, or straighten a curled-up rug corner in their path. Having a glimpse of what someone's going through can shift our whole posture toward them.

Naming some of these invisible burdens may open some needed conversations. Sometimes people fear they'll say the wrong thing, so they decide to say nothing at all. We're all going to have to give each other some grace as we move forward into community alive with kingdom fullness.

If you need to engage in a conversation that may or may not be hard, or that may be hard for you, here are some essential habits:

- Prayer. This isn't five minutes of prayer. This is consistent prayer over hours and days. Living in community will stretch your prayer life, but living in a healthy community as the body of Christ depends on a rich life of prayer. Prayer is an essential part of this process.

- Finding mentors, coaches, accountability partners, and trusted colleagues. We all have areas where we lack self-awareness about ourselves. Mature mentors and coaches help us sort essentials from non-essentials; they help us stay honest about our motives. They provide much-needed perspective.

- Committing ahead of time to keep scope limited. If you engage in a hard conversation, it's not the time to throw in "everything and the kitchen sink." Stay clear, factual, generous in your assumptions, and limited to your specific scope.

- Exercising respect and non-defensiveness. If you engage in a hard conversation, protect the confidence of others and speak only for yourself. Notice and manage any default responses you have: whether your gut reaction is cynicism, pride, fear, shame, resentment, defensiveness, or conflict-avoidant rather than truth-pursuing.

- Practicing non-anxious responses to expressions of anger. If you engage in a hard conversation and anger is expressed, consider whether the anger is ego-driven or whether it may be rightly informed righteous anger. God is also angered by injustice. Anger itself is not a sin; it can be a response to frustration, pain, fear, or trauma. When someone is angry, practice establishing a non-anxious presence to listen to what's behind the anger.

- Be ready to extend grace to those on the journey and who are learning.

We don't have to fear the sting of hard conversations: "There is no fear in love. But perfect love drives out fear because fear has to do with punishment. The one who fears is not made perfect in love" (1 John 4:8).

We're all going to have to give each other some grace as we move forward into community alive with kingdom fullness.

Navigating Hard Conversations: Coaching for Church Leaders Who Are Women

In my coaching and training work with pastors who are women, similar questions frequently arise. While every situation is unique, these are some of my common practices and principles I implement and share with church leaders who are women.

When I'm coaching pastors who've carried a hard load because they are women, I acknowledge their wounds and the offenses against them and name what to do with it (take it to Jesus). I affirm that the toll of trauma is real and legitimate. I don't belittle their experiences.

Healthy healing means noticing any tendency toward denial. I encourage leaders to practice honesty by feeling what they're grieving, not numbing it. It's healthy to grieve sin, injustice, and wrongdoing. We shouldn't be comfortable with spiritual malpractice. A woman carried the Messiah; Jesus had no patience for the mistreatment of women, and mistreatment hurts our mission to reach the lost.

I encourage women I'm coaching to grieve and lament in healthy ways, by submitting to Jesus and surrendering anger, fear, and sadness to him. I pray they receive healing and cleansing from Jesus, resting in him so they are free to forgive even when reconciliation is not possible, and so that they don't grow a root of bitterness or lose their joy. I also urge women leaders to pursue safe spaces to vent and lay down frustrations and the pain of an experience, so it doesn't infect their relationships with their brothers in Christ and even with other sisters going through similar experiences.

I also encourage them to connect with mentors. I know that for me, mentors can gently redirect my attention and bring me back to the feet of Jesus. They lament with me, encourage me with the Word, and help me see when I need to forgive and when I've grieved enough and it's time to move forward. Experienced mentors can help clarify your reactions, because there may be times you assume challenging interactions are because you're a woman when that's not the case. If your character needs to mature or you're bringing toxic habits into your environment, your challenges aren't because you're a woman, and a godly mentor knows how to help you grow.

Through all this, I encourage women in leadership to rest in their identity in Christ; you are a child of God first, a pastor second. You're not a victim: you are more than a conqueror. Your call is from God and for God. Frequently, I offer women additional counsel, like:

- Keep your heart soft and your skin thick. "Be wise as a serpent, innocent as a dove" (Matt 10:16).

- Sometimes, it's personal; other times it feels personal but isn't. A challenging interaction may reflect a particular mindset of a group of people who may direct it at you but would also apply it to anyone else in the pulpit.

- When a setting feels awkward or you don't feel welcomed into an all-male group, they're not necessarily against you. Sometimes they simply don't know what to do with the culture shift; it's been all-male so long it's unintentionally become exclusive. As Dr. Jim Lo once commented, "people don't know what to do with you, but that's okay because God does. Stick it out."

- Don't apologize for any shift in dynamics created because of your presence. If God has called you to be there, the group is better for it. Keep your head up and get to work with God-confidence.

- Don't schedule a business meeting by asking, "are you okay meeting with me alone or in public?" Offer options within your boundaries and respond to what is reciprocated. When we start by asking the question, it puts it on the radar when it may not have been an issue.

- Consider the practicalities of how to shift the culture around you. At gatherings, rather than clumping together, spread out, and sit at different tables; it gives men the opportunity to experience working with women as colleagues and keeps the atmosphere kingdom oriented.

Depending on temperament, consider stepping into hard conversations and asking pastors who are men about their experiences, concerns, and questions; listen deeply. When your heart is in a healthy place, you can find opportunities to disciple within that space. (We can't love someone we despise, and we can't disciple someone we don't love). As experience, mental health, and maturity allow, it's valuable to create safe spaces for co-laborers who are men to be heard and listened to, where they can ask hard questions (even and especially those questions that potentially sound sexist when said out loud). Through word and action, our spiritual brothers need to know we're not going to flippantly "cancel" them because they unintentionally offend. But while we are committed to loving them unconditionally, part of that is investing in their discipleship to the level of their willingness.

Women need to continue speaking up. Nothing changes if women avoid bringing our experiences into the light. It's not healthy for the church (or men) if women suppress the truth. Often, women will need to initiate the conversation; it rarely comes to us.

Whenever there are circumstances when women are belittled or discouraged from following God's call, it can be hard to remember sometimes that other leaders with influence may find you intimidating.

One time, a dear colleague shared he was apprehensive about having a phone call with me to engage in a difficult conversation. He said, "I thought you were going to yell at me for asking that question at the conference session!" I applauded his bravery, expressed my appreciation for him, and invited him into a "safe place" conversation.

Navigating Hard Conversations: Coaching for Church Leaders Who Are Men

It's a privilege to help pastors and church leaders who are men to navigate the dynamics of co-laboring with women for kingdom fullness. There are many honest, committed men proactively engaged in learning how to celebrate and support leaders who are women. In training and coaching settings, common questions emerge. These are some of the principles and practices I share with church leaders who are men:

- If there are ways women in leadership have treated you unfairly, spoken unkindly about your ministry, made you feel like a liability, or belittled your genuine questions, that's not right, and it's okay to say so. Each leader should be striving to live up to the call of God. Not all denominations have the same degree or kinds of challenges among men and women in pastoral ministry. There are times when men who support women in pastoral ministry aren't treated fairly by women in leadership in their denominations. When that happens, forgive, even if reconciliation isn't an option.

- Reckon with the regular experiences women navigate while attempting to follow God's call. To recap examples from earlier chapters, these may include remarks on appearance, hormones, children, marriage, and current or potential pregnancy; hostile comments such as, "We're praying your church will close because you're a woman leading in sin," and derogatory or stereotyping language like "girl," "b*tch," "little lady", or "sweetheart," as well as cheap, dismissive labels difficult to escape: "emotional," "angry," "feminist,"[1] or "bitter"; and the no-win dynamic of being "the exception" —when hard-won acceptance is still approached as an exception to the rule: "She's alright, though."

- Decide ahead of time ways you can respond if you're in a situation where you hear colleagues who are men speaking in ways that fail to honor Christ or demonstrate respect for your sisters. Ask God to give you insight into winsome ways you can handle challenging settings and how to respond in ways that will reflect your values of living into kingdom fullness.

- Ask pastors who are women about their experiences; listen deeply, ask follow-up questions, and invite the Holy Spirit to show you how to respond over the long haul. Notice who is missing: if women who'd been preparing for ministry "dropped off the radar," follow up with them and find out where or if they're active in ministry and why or why not.

- The tone and content of presentations or conversations at conferences or seminars should be consistent regardless of who is present in the room. We speak as a holy people; inappropriate remarks create an unhealthy and unwelcoming environment for all. It then (often unintentionally) also becomes awkward for women to step into that space.

- If the Holy Spirit convicts you of your speech, behavior, or attitudes towards a woman or women in kingdom fullness, repent, and if possible, reconcile and make amends.

- Pray and evaluate if you truly believe in the scriptural vision for kingdom fullness, including women in all roles of ministry leadership. Weigh whether your actions, attitudes, and words demonstrate your values. (For example, how many times last year did a clergywoman preach? Who are some of the women you are mentoring or coaching? In all areas, show and live your belief in kingdom fullness and women in ministry leadership.)

- For healthy kingdom flourishing, men need to lead and follow both men and women; women need to lead and follow both men and women.

Through the power of the Holy Spirit, in Jesus' name, women and men can engage in hard conversations with both reverence for the presence of God in our midst and confidence in Christ, the head of the body of Christ. By receiving each others' invisible burdens, responding with grace, practicing intentional habits and postures, and applying the wisdom of mentors and coaches, we are equipped to enter hard conversations with prayer, compassion, generosity, humility, wisdom, curiosity, conviction, and openness. *God is within her; she will not fall.*

Together, we can invite the Holy Spirit to knit us together in bold, holy witness as we carry each other's burdens. "Very truly I tell you, no servant is greater than his master, nor is a messenger greater than the one who sent him. A new command I give you: Love one another. As I have loved you, so you must love one another. By this, everyone will know that you are my disciples, if you love one another" (John 13:16, 34-35).

Come, Holy Spirit. We invite you into our interactions. Where there is hesitancy, grow trust. Where we've fallen short in how we approach each other and how we approach You, forgive us, and give us the tools and insight to go forward in healthy ways that honor You. Let our interactions be a beautiful witness to Your goodness.

Chapter Eleven Discussion Questions

Rev. Santes Beatty, Director of Next Gen Ministries for The Wesleyan Church

1. What ways do you see the tensions around invisible burdens as invitations to intercede for others? What would a commitment to intercede for others look like for you?

2. Which burdens do you most identify with and why? How can you find a safe place to process them?

3. Which burdens surprised you, were difficult to understand, or needed more clarity? How can you find a safe place to process them?

4. When have you seen a hard conversation end well? What were some of the characteristics, tools, or takeaways that you think apply to this conversation?

5. As discussed in this chapter, some habits help to shape healthy hard conversations. Which of these habits do you need to practice more regularly?

6. Who do you go to when you need to check in about something you experienced or said? Does someone have permission to not only encourage you but also challenge you and spur you on towards good things? How do you find those individuals if you don't have them in your life currently?

7. The efforts to "Decide, Describe, and Practice" were mentioned more than once in this chapter. Which of these come more easily for you, and which ones are the most difficult?

8. Is there a burning question you need to process with others concerning this chapter?

9. If you could summarize this chapter in 1-2 sentences, what would they be?

10. Would someone you know benefit from the information you learned about in this chapter? Who needs to hear about what you learned?

This Week

Set aside time each day to pray over a challenging relationship, situation, or dynamic.

CHAPTER TWELVE

How Good It Can Be: Living the Vision

*"I want to know Christ—yes, to know the power of his
resurrection and participation in his sufferings, becoming like him in his death, and so, somehow, attaining to
the resurrection from the dead. Not that I have already
obtained all this, or have already arrived at my goal,* but I
press on to take hold of that for which Christ Jesus took
hold of me. *Brothers and sisters, I do not consider myself
yet to have taken hold of it. But one thing I do: Forgetting
what is behind and straining toward what is ahead, I press
on toward the goal to win the prize for which God has
called me heavenward in Christ Jesus" (Phil. 3:10-14).*

Sometimes Christians talk about the kingdom of God being
here "already" but "not yet" at the same time. When you read
through the Gospels, you see God's inbreaking kingdom active in
the life of Jesus Christ: sick people healed, hungry people full, rag-
ing seas stilled. Through the Holy Spirit, God's kingdom continues
to break into our world, changing and transforming lives. At the
same time, we know it's not yet completely here. We don't yet live

face-to-face with Jesus in eternity; there is still suffering, brokenness, sin, pain, loss, and death. We're in-between: following Jesus
through the power of the Holy Spirit, sharing the good news with
our hurting world. The body of Christ sometimes falls short of who
God calls, equips, and empowers us to be.

That doesn't change who God calls, equips, and empowers us
to be. We are still called to work together as the body of Christ,
co-laboring for the kingdom of God in the fullness of our calling.
And we "press on to take hold of that for which Christ Jesus took
hold" of us. The power of the Holy Spirit will not let us settle. God
entrusts us with the vision of the kingdom of God. While we live in
the real circumstances and challenges of today, we also live in the
revealed promises, power, and presence of God. We don't stop at
diagnosing the dysfunction and deficiency in the body of Christ;
we receive and wrestle with and contend for the vision of a flourishing body that God gives us in scripture and empowers us to live in
the present.

This means you and I aren't surprised when there are challenges, and we aren't surprised when God shows up powerfully to
call us to live more deeply into his vision for his church. Today's
hurdles are real; the revelation of God's intent for humanity is
also real, and the Holy Spirit's call to sanctified living is real.
When we live toward God's vision for the body of Christ, God is
faithful to show us in new ways just how much we all must rely
on his power.

One of my mentors helped me see how to walk in this reality. As
I've mentioned, I coach and teach in a lot of different spaces. At one
point, some event organizers scheduled me to speak at an event.
I'd already started working on my presentation when the organizers
communicated, I was being released from the engagement. They'd
received pushback when the event schedule listed a woman on the

speaking lineup, so they chose to respond to the criticism by "going in a different direction."

When I expressed my frustration over this to a mentor, my mentor responded, "…but did that surprise you? Were you expecting something different?" She wasn't urging me to be a pessimist; she was urging me not to be surprised by challenges—and not to be surprised by God's faithfulness through them.

These words echo the wisdom for all believers in 1 Peter 4:12-16: "Dear friends, do not be surprised at the fiery ordeal that has come on you to test you, as though something strange was happening to you. But rejoice inasmuch as you participate in the sufferings of Christ, so that you may be overjoyed when his glory is revealed. If you are insulted because of the name of Christ, you are blessed, for the Spirit of glory and of God rests on you. If you suffer, it should not be as a murderer or thief or any other kind of criminal, or even as a meddler. However, if you suffer as a Christian, do not be ashamed, but praise God that you bear that name."

Some of our sisters and brothers around the world are required to meet in secret to worship; they can be arrested for worshiping together or owning a Bible. I don't know persecution like that. You don't have to be familiar with that level of persecution to receive the wisdom from this scripture: brothers and sisters, *don't be surprised when following Jesus costs you something.* Don't be ashamed or embarrassed that you're going through hardship when hardship shows up specifically because you're trying to obey and follow Jesus Christ.

My mentor's reminder pointed me toward realistic expectations of the kind of resistance I was likely to encounter. Accepting the likelihood of a situation like that doesn't mean I accept the situation itself as somehow alright. But when I'm not surprised by that kind of situation, I'm free to spend my energy more deliberately and productively toward God's vision for the body of Christ and my calling in it.

When we name challenges with clarity, we can accept the reality of what we're dealing with. When we've acknowledged the reality of the challenge, the Holy Spirit can begin to inspire and empower our imaginations to be good stewards of the gap between the dysfunction in the body of Christ and God's revealed vision for the body of Christ. Living toward the vision doesn't require us to be pessimistic about these challenges or to be in denial about them either. Living toward the vision puts each hurdle in perspective and shapes and defines our response.

Perspective Shaped by Vision

When you and I choose to pray and live into God's vision for the church, it takes time. Sometimes it takes identifying and implementing practical steps with forward-looking faith. Sometimes it takes focus in the middle of seemingly competing demands. It takes prayer as we discern where God's vision ends and human solutions or motivations begin. It takes joy to celebrate milestones along the way, especially in the face of hurdles. And living into the vision takes community as God enlivens this vision through the gift of each others' presence, ideas, insights, and gifts.

In medicine, sometimes doctors care for patients whose progress is incremental. For example, when someone has extensive knee surgery, care doesn't end when the operation is over; it's just beginning. Physicians and patients work together step by step in practical ways toward a specific goal.

Sometimes, patients connect challenging goals with a vision of meaningful experiences in their lives. A patient may have a specific physical therapy goal after surgery: "so I can hike my favorite trail again" or "so I can get down on the floor with my grandkids."

Sometimes the vision is simple and stark: a patient needs to meet milestones, "so I can try to walk again" or "so I can try to live independently." Anyone who's had a knee replacement knows how much work goes into gaining just one more degree of mobility with the new joint.

Connecting with a patient's "why" helps them keep going when it gets tough; it helps physical therapists and nurses know how best to come alongside someone in their recovery and rehabilitation. It's easier to keep perspective during a difficult physical therapy session when you remember your "why." That vision, that goal shapes your perspective in the middle of a recovery or strengthening process that can be slow, painful, frustrating, and exhausting.

Remembering your "why" is also a helpful habit when you're a pastor trying to persist around hurdles or when you're a church leader asking the Holy Spirit to transform your organization toward God's dream for the body of Christ.

Here are some questions to reflect on as you steward the opportunity to live into God's vision for the church:

- What do data and statistics show about where your church (or district or denomination) is right now—really? (You have to be realistic about your starting point.)

- Where is God calling you to be? (How might the Holy Spirit be convicting you?)

- What steps could help you get from here to there? (Community and wise mentors are a gift for discerning pragmatic possibilities.)

- What's your "why"? "So that I/we can _____..." (What specific gifts, joys, and burdens do you sense God placing on your heart as you discern your unique individual or organizational calling within the body of Christ?)

As you or your small group, congregation, district, or denomination wrestle with the first question (what the data shows about where you are now), maybe a mental picture will be helpful as you realistically assess where you're starting from.

It sounds a little like home organizer Marie Kondo.

When she first visits a cluttered home overflowing with belongings and chats with its overwhelmed inhabitants, she asks them to pile all their clothing on a bed or surface so they can see everything they have: their clothes, everything from dressers, closets, storage closets; all of it. When people see it all in one big pile, it becomes visually obvious they have much more than they wear or need. With that simple, forceful visual, it becomes easier for them to begin sorting. But first, they must pile up their clothing and acknowledge how much there is: the starting point is reality.

As we face the reality of where we are, God is ready to meet us and win us toward the vision revealed in scripture and empowered by the Holy Spirit. When the Holy Spirit convicts us about how we're falling short of that vision, we can respond by looking for ways to take steps toward it.

And when the going gets tough, it's helpful to remember your "why," your "so that…"

So that you can follow God's call to pursue ordained pastoral ministry?

So that you can begin designing incremental steps to reframe recruiting processes so that they seek out, retain, and celebrate the whole body of Christ?

So that pulpits don't stand empty while women can't find churches that will hire them?

So that our called daughters and nieces and sisters and friends and moms and aunts are free to follow God's calling knowing that within their denomination, they'll find deliberate, organized, prompt encouragement?

So that the Gospel will be preached by more people in more places reaching more souls?

So that we can reach people with the love, grace, hope, and joy of Jesus Christ in a tired, disillusioned, angry, competitive world?

So that we steward our heritage of women preachers in the 1800s and early 1900s—women lay, licensed, and ordained preachers who traveled by horse in the cold and heat?

So that we honor our heritage of women preachers who proclaimed the full Gospel of salvation and sanctification in churches, on street corners, in red light districts and in camp meetings all over the United States and in many places around the world?

So that we praise God for our heritage of women preachers showing up and revivals breaking out?

So that we give thanks for the men and women who were saved and sanctified, congregations planted with nothing but a tent and a handful of people because of women who said "yes" to God?

How is God calling us to receive his vision?

Are our imaginations too small?

Why do we care what anyone else thinks of us? In my Wesleyan Methodist holiness tradition, being different wasn't a "bug" in the design, it was a feature! The Salvation Army started as "fringe;" they got beat up and sometimes arrested for street preaching. People who are obsessively committed to Christ's vision will never fit in with others around them. Not since the disciples walked the earth and not now.

There is no witness like the witness of preaching with mud on your face. There is no vision like the vision of Christ to steer us through the mud and proclaim the Gospel anyway.

In the 1870s and 1880s a woman named Sarah Cooke traveled as a Free Methodist lay preacher with a group of men and women from a variety of traditions (including Baptist!). This small group traveled to towns in Indiana, Michigan, Wisconsin, Illinois, and more, visiting, praying, and preaching. In her book *Wayside Sketches*, she describes a situation in Battle Creek, Michigan:

> The Salvation Army had landed at Battle Creek, Mich. The devil was stirred, and determined they should have no foothold there. After they were thrown into a stream of water, three of them left, but one remained. He was put into prison, dragged through the filth of the street, his face covered with mud; but he still glorified God, and, taking his stand on the sidewalk, he preached "the unsearchable riches of Christ;" and as he talked the glory of God shone on him, and three thousand people gazed in wonder on that face, shining as did the face of Moses when he came down from the mount of God. [1]

There is no witness like the witness of preaching with mud on your face. There is no vision like the vision of Christ to steer us through the mud and proclaim the Gospel anyway.

> What, then, shall we say in response to these things? If God is for us, who can be against us? He who did not spare his own Son, but gave him up for us all— how will he not also, along with him, graciously give us all things? Who will bring any charge against those whom God has chosen? It is God who justifies. Who then is the one who condemns? No one. Christ Jesus

who died—more than that, who was raised to life—
is at the right hand of God and is also interceding for
us. Who shall separate us from the love of Christ?
Shall trouble or hardship or persecution or famine or
nakedness or danger or sword? As it is written: "For
your sake we face death all day long; we are considered
as sheep to be slaughtered." No, in all these things we
are more than conquerors through him who loved us
(Rom. 8:31-37).

When you're tempted to focus on the hurdles over the hope,
dwell on how faithful God has been in the past: the same God who's
with you and me today. The enemy wants to discourage: to drain
our courage, to create a pause, to make us reevaluate. But when I
witness God's faithfulness to my sisters and brothers in the past and
today, I am encouraged, strengthened for the work at hand.

When I dwell on God's goodness and faithfulness to his people
throughout scripture, across history, right down into my personal
life, I'm reminded that God always cares more about what's being
done in me than what's being done through me. Part of God's faithfulness is shaping us into who we need to be to receive God's calling
and vision. God is faithful to work in our hearts as individuals, as
congregations, and as denominations.

When the vision seems distant or the hits start to add up, the
Holy Spirit walks with us to shape perspective even in the middle
of harm, even while learning to catalyze those negative experiences.
If God hasn't called me, nothing will work. If God hasn't called you,
nothing will work. All I can do is continue to be me, for God.

Be you, for God.

When you dwell in gratitude for the Holy Spirit's victories, it
keeps the vision in focus. When someone comes to the Lord, or

when an antagonist shifts from excluding to championing, those are things you can't force or manufacture. That's God's grace at work. When you stay rooted in God's Word, the Holy Spirit will draw a line from God's faithfulness to believers then, right to God's faithfulness to believers now. The Holy Spirit can mend divides that can only be healed with God's grace and love.

I don't want to tell Jesus what is and isn't possible! By celebrating the work of God, our imaginations are renewed as the Holy Spirit prompts us to receive God's picture for the body and direct our energy toward it.

Kingdom fullness means expecting to see God's promises come to life in unexpected ways—here, now, today.

God may be asking you to dream a "God-sized" dream that will fail without his intervention. This requires you to surrender it all.

In the same breath, if God asks you to dream something small or obscure or forgettable or weird, are you still willing? This requires the same surrender. This is kingdom fullness, too.

Where the Holy Spirit stings and we refuse to numb conviction, we are living the way of kingdom fullness; we're living surrender. Following Jesus isn't more complicated than a towel and basin.

The vision we're holding in our hands is not one of mechanical, rigid legalism: checking a box, counting how many women are on a platform or podcast. The vision God reveals in scripture costs more than that.

Legalism is easy, something we can do with our own effort. The Holy Spirit invites us onto the harder path of surrender.

It is the Holy Spirit who indwells us, unites us, calls us, empowers us, and marks us for ministry roles. "There is neither Jew nor Gentile, neither slave nor free, nor is there male and female, for you are all one in Christ Jesus" (Gal. 3:28).

Implementing the Vision: Unleashing the Gifts of Half the Body

This week, this month, this year, how can we pursue and implement God's revealed vision together? We can:

- Pray: Following the Holy Spirit, we invite God to stir our hearts.
- Partner: No one welcomes God's vision for the body of Christ in isolation.
- Persist: When we labor in prayer and partner for the Gospel, we're free to persist.

As Rev. Dr. Anita Eastlack tells me, "Heaven is counting on us to be 'plan A' to reach the world. Time is short and Jesus needs all his daughters and sons to be fully engaged side by side, bringing the good news of Jesus. Let's believe this is possible and is God's will and do the hard work to make it work."

How can we implement God's vision for the body of Christ? Dr. Eastlack and Rev. Zack Coffin developed three factors to consider. As men and women co-labor in God's kingdom, three things need to be in alignment for the sake of a congregation, group, or denomination's integrity: our position, our posture, and our practice.

In denominations that support the ordination of women, what should that look like?

- Our position: We ordain women and have an egalitarian theology.
- Our posture: Professional mutual respect.
- Our practice: Consistent and aligned with position and posture.

We consistently lose sight of God's vision when those three defining characteristics are misaligned with each other. Position alone doesn't implement God's vision for the church. Each of these three are essential to embrace kingdom fullness. Where practice is inconsistent and misaligned, we are not fully living our position, even if our position echoes God's vision. Where practice is consistent and aligned with posture and position, God's kingdom breaks loose.

Earlier, I suggested that we don't stop at diagnosing dysfunction and deficiency in the body; we receive and wrestle with and contend for the vision of a flourishing body that God gives us in scripture and empowers us to live in the present. "What, then, shall we say in response to these things? If God is for us, who can be against us?"

Come, Holy Spirit. Forgive us for being easily distracted from Your vision for the body of Christ. We want the boldness of preachers who bear witness with mud on their faces. We want the anointing that empowers us after being tossed in a creek to stand up in wet shoes and proclaim the good news of Jesus Christ. We want our position, posture, and practice to be aligned because we desperately need You; our world desperately needs You. Our countries, states, and towns desperately need You. Where there is violence, addiction, despair, hopelessness, lack— what town doesn't have those? —everywhere there is brokenness, pour out Your Holy Spirit on Your sons and daughters, to preach the promise and hope of the good news of Jesus Christ. Let us be bold for the vision of Your kingdom. Amen.

Chapter Twelve Reflection & Discussion Questions

Pastor Marv LaLone, Church Planter and Lead Pastor of
Good News Church, Michigan

I first met Katie and Randy at an Exponential Conference when I was exploring a call to church planting. A few months later, she led sections of a Church Planting Essentials cohort I had joined. During that training I sensed the Lord leading me, so I asked Katie to prayerfully consider being my church planting coach. That was in 2020, and she has been my coach ever since. We're colleagues, friends, and co-laborers on a mission to be a small part of multiplying God's kingdom, and, above all else, we are brother and sister in Christ. This can work and we can flourish together.

In four years of coaching, Katie has been a source of wisdom from the Holy Spirit, has challenged me when I was off-course, held me accountable to what I said I would do, and encouraged me when I was ready to quit. She has helped my family and me navigate some very difficult situations in life and ministry, and I am a better leader and a better disciple of Jesus for it. Kingdom fullness is within reach if you're willing to stretch for it.

Discussion Questions

1. *Imagine yourself working in a ministry with men and women together at every level of leadership (kingdom fullness), giving and receiving direction from each other, collaborating in groups and one-on-one. Does this cause tension for you? Where does that tension come from? Is your immediate reaction positive or negative? Why do you think that is?*

2. Prayerfully consider how God may be asking you to address the source of that tension with him in a transformative way.

3. As you've identified challenges in your inner life, as well as practical outward challenges, what is one simple step you can take to overcome each challenge? What does this look like in your context?

4. If you are in a denomination or group that supports the ordination of women, are you personally or organizationally aligned in your position, practice, and posture? If not, what changes need to be made to get there?

5. What is your next faithful step?

This Week

Seek out examples from the past that will help encourage and inspire you with their persistence for kingdom fullness.

CONCLUSION

An Anointed Body: Running the Race

"Then Jesus came to them and said, 'All authority in heaven and on earth has been given to me. Therefore, go and make disciples of all nations, baptizing them in the name of the Father and of the Son and of the Holy Spirit, and teaching them to obey everything I have commanded you. And surely I am with you always, to the very end of the age'"
(Matt. 28:18-20).

When Mary, Salome, Joanna, Mary Magdalene, and other disciples walked to Jesus' tomb, they carried spices with them to care for his dead body. It was one last thing they could do for their teacher. It was an act of love; it was practical and extravagant at the same time. Joanna's husband worked for Herod; Herod, who was part of why Jesus' body was in the tomb. They went to perform burial practices on the body of Christ (broken for them).

Laying out a body is a task that's both practical and reverent. It's something I did as a nurse. I know the pragmatic realities of death. Some things, like funerary practices, change with time or culture. Some realities of the dead are unchanging.

This group of women showed up to attend to the practicalities of death, to honor Jesus, to share their grief and show their devotion. After a humiliating execution, his body would not go uncared for.

These disciples thought the corpse of Christ needed the spices of the graveyard.

The body of Christ wasn't done.

I've never had to erase medical paperwork to alter "time of death" to "never mind, patient alive after three days in the morgue."

I'm not ready to call "time of death" on the church, the body of Christ, either.

Jesus' physical body wasn't done then and the church, the body of Christ, isn't done now.

God is within her; she will not fall.

The Holy Spirit poured out life on over one hundred men and women gathered together praying in the upper room.

We're not anointing a body for burial.

We're receiving the sweet anointing of the Holy Spirit to live as Christ's body until Jesus returns and all things are made new.

Jesus didn't stay in the tomb. He showed his scars to his disciples, ate fish, and surprised disciples in an Emmaus home.

And no matter how wrong the church gets it, no matter how discouraging it may be to see how the daughters of those first spice-bearers are treated sometimes, God did not abandon Jesus to the grave, and God has not abandoned the body of Christ to defeat.

Sisters, we stand in the long line of women who preached the good news of the resurrection of Jesus Christ, all the way from the empty tomb to where you sit today. You are the daughters of Salome and Joanna, Mary the mother of James and Mary Magdalene. We can all put our burial plans away; the embalming spices aren't needed. The body of Christ doesn't need our grave cloths.

God entrusted women with the good news of the resurrection of Jesus Christ, the first fruit of the resurrection of the dead.

No one could keep him buried and no one can bury you, either.

This is not because of some motivational poster about how unsinkable you are.

It's because of the explosive life-giving power of the Holy Spirit and who God is.

The way you follow your calling may look different than you pictured, the place may be different than you assumed, the denominational name may vary, the shape of your vocation may be unfolding, but pay attention: there is no shame in walking away from a leader or group or denomination where you thought your gifts and calling would be welcomed and they were buried in the dirt instead.

But.

If you feel like you had to walk away from your entire calling at the same time, receive this: *God has not cancelled your calling.* The Holy Spirit hasn't hit "void" on your gifts. Closed doors aren't always from God.

Let me gently hold out some dangerous hope today: *hope that what those in power may have declared dead and done-for, God is resurrecting.*

You don't have to lay your hopes for your calling in a borrowed, second-hand tomb.

The church's vocation is not to call good things dead; the church's vocation is to speak life and light into the darkness.

God is within her; she will not fall.

There may be a deficiency in the body of Christ, there may be dysfunction, but the body of Christ is not dead, and the Holy Spirit is shaking us awake and asking if we truly want to be sanctified and alive in Christ.

When you and I proclaim the mystery of the faith—that Christ has died, Christ is risen, and Christ will come again—no power of hell, no principality or power, neither height nor depth, nothing can separate us from the love of God that is in Christ Jesus our Lord.

We do not preach any gospel but Jesus Christ. Trauma or confusion or the slow work of personal development may lead you to be uncertain of your voice for a while. *But ultimately, no power can steal your voice and make you stop testifying to the transforming grace of God.*

The Spirit who anointed Paul and Silas singing at the top of their lungs in a prison cell is the same Spirit who empowers you today. If the jailers couldn't shut up Paul and Silas, what, really, can an administrator do to you? If Jesus Christ has hidden the mystery of the Gospel in your heart and you cannot be at peace without proclaiming what God has done for you, don't let anyone stop you. Do what you need to do: check other denominations, find supportive organizations, stand on a box and preach on the street and in red-light districts like our sisters did 150 years ago. You will not answer to pastors or regional leaders for your gifts; you answer to Jesus Christ, who entrusted women with the good news of the resurrection.

In Wesleyan/holiness denominations, we come from a long line of women who proclaim the Word of God for the people of God. On February 25th, 1712, Susanna Wesley wrote to her husband, Rev. Samuel Wesley, responding to his letter. He'd been away traveling and had written to ask her to stop teaching scripture from the parsonage, because the church curate (assistant pastor) had written to the absent Rev. Samuel to complain, because Susanna's parsonage teaching drew larger crowds than the curate's church sermons did.

Susanna wrote to Samuel, "if you do, after all, think fit to dissolve this assembly, do not tell me that you desire me to do it, for that will not satisfy my conscience; but send me your positive command, in such full and express terms, *as may absolve me from all guilt and punishment for neglecting this opportunity of doing good,* when you and I shall appear before the great and awful tribunal of our Lord Jesus Christ." Rev. Wesley apparently was not prepared to answer to God for commanding her to stop and he never wrote on the matter again. Later, their son John took the extraordinary step of supporting Methodist women as lay preachers in an age when a lot of popular wisdom suggested it wasn't even worth teaching girls to read.

Who wants to answer to God when we "appear before the great and awful tribunal of our Lord Jesus Christ" for obstructing women from the opportunity of doing good? "If anyone, then, knows the good they ought to do and doesn't do it, it is sin for them" (James 4:17). Christians, do not lead us into the sin of neglecting the opportunity of doing good.

God is within her; she will not fall.

"Where, o death, is your victory? Where, o death, is your sting?" (I Cor. 15:55). Jesus Christ said, "I will build my church, and the gates of hell shall not prevail against it" (Matt. 16:18). The Holy Spirit who rushed through an upstairs gathering in Jerusalem is the same Spirit enlivening the church, the body of Christ, today.

God is within her; she will not fall.

Those spice-bearers ran. Those disciples in the graveyard dropped their expensive burial spices and ran to tell the others the tomb was empty, angels had appeared, another earthquake had hit; those women ran to share the good news of the resurrected Christ. They ran to preach the Gospel. They ran.

I've got my running shoes on.

I'm ready to run.

I'm ready to preach the good news of Jesus Christ.

I'm ready to follow Mary and Salome and Mary M. and Joanna. Their footprints always lead to Jesus.

"Therefore, since we are surrounded by such a great cloud of witnesses, let us throw off everything that hinders and the sin that so easily entangles. And let us run with perseverance the race marked out for us, fixing our eyes on Jesus, the pioneer and perfecter of faith. For the joy set before him he endured the cross, scorning its shame, and sat down at the right hand of the throne of God" (Hebrews 12:1-2).

I have one question for my sisters and brothers.

Are your shoes on?

Are you ready to run with the good news?

Are you ready to walk with the good news, like Jesus walked with disciples whose hearts burned within them on the way to Emmaus?

Some of us wheel the good news, pushing strollers, in wheelchairs, on skateboards or scooters.

However you get from one place to another, we move best when we move together.

Tag.

You're "it."

Conclusion Reflection & Discussion Questions

Rev. Jervie Windom, Lead Pastor of Resonate Church, Texas

This book challenged me to ask these questions of myself and to pray this prayer. I need to keep my eyes on this and remember to be intentional in my discipleship of others. Will you pray along with me?

"Loving God, we approach You with extreme gratitude for the opportunity to serve alongside our brothers and sisters in Christ. We thank You for the unique gifts and perspectives each of us brings to the body of Christ by Your design. As we reflect on the power of collaboration in our faith journeys and ministries, we ask for Your guidance and wisdom. Teach us to encourage and support one another, celebrating our diverse talents and unique gifts. We acknowledge our challenges when working together and ask Your Holy Spirit to guide us through these times. Help us foster an environment where every believer is empowered to serve and where ministries become accurate reflections of Your love. Continue to shape us and deepen our understanding of Your purpose for Your diverse family of faith. May we mature in holiness, walking humbly and lovingly with one another as we advance Your kingdom and share the Gospel with the world. In the name of Jesus Christ, we pray. Amen."

Discussion Questions

1. *In what ways have you experienced the power of collaboration within your own faith journey and ministry?*
2. *How can we encourage and support one another's unique gifts within the body of Christ?*

3. *What challenges do you face when working alongside fellow believers, and how can you rely on the Holy Spirit's guidance to navigate these difficulties?*

4. *How can you personally strive to foster a more empowering environment for all believers, regardless of gender, to serve in ministry?*

5. *In what ways can you continue to mature in holiness and deepen your understanding of God's purpose for the diverse family of faith?*

This Week:

Be you, for God.

ACKNOWLEDGMENTS

This book has been shaped by an extraordinary number of women and men who generously gave their time, attention, and heart to this project. I am profoundly grateful for the valuable insights contributed by the multi-denominational community of faith. It's been a privilege to interview hundreds of pastors and church leaders and to engage with hundreds more at conferences and workshop sessions. They gave me the gift of their honesty, vulnerability, and trust, and their insights are a gift to readers throughout these pages.

Leaders from denominational and academic contexts contributed timely wisdom. Early chapter readers provided valuable feedback at critical stages, and I'm deeply thankful for the expertise and coaching from Rev. David Drury. The generous and thoughtful forewords by Rev. Dr. Ed Love and General Superintendent Emerita Rev. Dr. Jo Anne Lyon shaped the opening of this book; additionally, a variety of church leaders, writers, pastors, and scholars contributed reflections and discussion questions to shape the conclusion of each chapter. I am thankful for the voices of Elizabeth Glass Turner, Pastor Jordan Loman, Rev. Dr. Andrea Summers, Rev. Dr. Ken Schenck, Rev. Dr. Tamar Eisenmann, Rev. Dr. Tanya Nace, Umfundisi Jim Lo, Rev. Zach Coffin, Rev. Dr. Anita Eastlack, Pastor Randy Lance, Rev. Santes Beatty, Rev. Marv LaLone, and Rev.

Jervie Windom. In a wonderful wrap-up, Susie Schaefer's publication team carried this project over the finish line.

I am also indebted to those prayer warriors, mentors, and colleagues who shaped my thinking, helped me process my experiences and equipped me to help others, who ministered to my heart and carried me to the feet of Jesus, who faithfully gave wise counsel, prayer support, and proved by life and ministry example that men and women working together in holiness truly is possible. I abide more deeply in Christ because of you: Dr. Anita Eastlack, Dr. Jo Anne Lyon, Dr. Jim Lo, Hank and my brothers and sisters of Thrive Church, Natasha V., Dr. Tim Roehl, Pastor Randy Lance, Julie, Pastor Marv and Robyn LaLone, and Ingri Tutu.

With my deepest gratitude and admiration, I thank my book doula, editor, colleague and friend Elizabeth Glass Turner. This project would not have been possible without her. I thank God that he brought us together for such a time and purpose as this. His timing is perfect, and his grace is always enough.

Finally, Team Lance: I am eternally grateful to my husband, brother in Christ, and partner in ministry, Randy. He so often believed in me before I believed in myself and sacrificially supported my calling in each season to serve God and his people. All my love to our boys, Simon and Levi. It is the joy of my life to stand side by side with Randy, guiding them as they grow into godly men. My cup runs over.

ABOUT THE AUTHOR

 Rev. Katie Lance is the Director of Discipleship for The Wesleyan Church. An ordained minister, Katie is passionate about coaching, equipping, and mobilizing lay leaders and pastors to multiply disciple-making movements. She gained valuable experience throughout fifteen years in church planting. She and her husband, Pastor Randy Lance, co-planted Thrive Church, where she ministered as lead pastor. Katie coaches pastors and leaders in multiple denominations and is a sought-after keynote speaker and workshop facilitator.

Katie came to the Christian faith as an adult. Before stepping into full-time ministry, she worked as a registered nurse in cardiac and intensive care units and still maintains her license as a registered nurse (RN). Her personal and professional background provides her with unique insight into kingdom challenges and opportunities in the church today.

Katie's greatest source of joy is spending time with her husband of twenty years and their teen boys, Simon and Levi. As a family they enjoy traveling, music and the arts, and anything that brings laughter together.

END NOTES

Chapter One - The Holy Spirit Can't Move Until You Do

1. All scripture references are NIV unless otherwise noted.
2. The Wesleyan Church
3. Julia A. J. Foote, "A Brand Plucked from the Fire: An Autobiographical Sketch" (2019). *Heritage Material.* 169. https://place.asburyseminary.edu/firstfruitsheritagematerial/169, p.7
4. Julia A. J. Foote, "A Brand Plucked from the Fire: An Autobiographical Sketch" (2019). *Heritage Material.* 169. https://place.asburyseminary.edu/firstfruitsheritagematerial/169, p. 112
5. Courtney Dunn, "The Importance of Stories for Cultivating a Culture of Women Leading in Ministry," 2020, https://www.thesacredalliance.org/scholars-collective-1 . Retrieved 8/31/23.

Chapter Two - Diagnosing the Body

1. See "Wesleyan Clergy Compensation Report" (Department of Education and Clergy Development of The Wesleyan Church, 2022), citing a 2018 Matt Bloom study.

Chapter Three - Missing Out: Hurdles to Discerning Kingdom-Full Vocation

1. Rob Dixon, *Together in Ministry: Women and Men in Flourishing Partnerships* (InterVarsity Press, 2021).

2. See "Wesleyan Clergy Compensation Report" (Department of Education and Clergy Development of The Wesleyan Church, 2022).

3. See "Wesleyan Clergy Compensation Report" (Department of Education and Clergy Development of The Wesleyan Church, 2022).

4. See Dr. Nijay Gupta, "Why I Believe in Women in Ministry Part 16: Junia Was a Prominent Female Apostle of the First Century Church," Crux Sola: Formed by Scripture to Live Like Christ, Patheos, 6/4/2019, https://www.patheos.com/blogs/cruxsola/2019/06/why-i-believe-in-women-in-ministry-part-16-gupta/.

Chapter Four - Catalyzing Leadership: Cultivating Kingdom Fullness

1. See several of N.T. Wright's works, including *Luke for Everyone* (London: Society for Promoting Christian Knowledge; Louisville: Westminster John Knox Press, 2004).

Chapter Five - Why the Wesleyan/Holiness Movement Settled for Less than Kingdom Fullness

1. See the pamphlet "Martin W. Knapp and Seth C. Rees: Two Pilgrims' Progress," by the late Dr. Lee Haines, former General Superintendent of The Wesleyan Church. A PDF of Dr.

Haines' pamphlet is accessible on the webpage www.wesleyan.org/our-wesleyan-heritage-247, retrieved 07/2023.

2. See Paul L. King's *Anointed Women: The Rich Heritage of Women in Ministry in the Christian & Missionary Alliance* (Word & Spirit Press, 2009).

3. See B.T. Roberts, *Ordaining Women: New Edition with Introduction and Notes*, Ed. by Benjamin D. Wayman (Eugene: Wipf & Stock, 2015).

4. Dr. Rebecca Laird, *Ordained Women in the Church of the Nazarene: The First Generation* (Kansas City: Nazarene Publishing House, 1993), *Introduction*

5. Dr. Lee M. Haines, "Women in Ministry: Challenging the Cultural Obstacles," Women in Ministry and Leadership Resource Center, The Wesleyan Church, retrieved August 2023, https://cdn.resources.wesleyan.org/wesleyanrc/wp-content/uploads/Women-in-Ministry-Cultural-Obstacles.pdf .

6. Dr. Rebecca Laird, *Ordained Women in the Church of the Nazarene: The First Generation* (Kansas City: Nazarene Publishing House, 1993)

7. Dr. Rebecca Laird, *Ordained Women in the Church of the Nazarene: The First Generation* (Kansas City: Nazarene Publishing House, 1993), *Introduction*

8. Maxine Haines and Lee M. Haines, *Celebrate Our Daughters: 150 Years of Women in Wesleyan Ministry* (Indianapolis: Wesleyan Publishing House, 2004), p. 325.

9. Maxine Haines and Lee M. Haines, *Celebrate Our Daughters: 150 Years of Women in Wesleyan Ministry* (Indianapolis: Wesleyan Publishing House, 2004), p. 326.

10. Lucille Sider Dayton and Donald Dayton, "Women in the Holiness Movement," originally presented in a seminar at the 1974 Christian Holiness Association convention, retrieved 8/21/23 from The Wesleyan Church Department of Education and Clergy Development: Women in Ministry Leadership, https://www.wesleyan.org/ecd/women-ministry-leadership, p. 23.

11. Lucille Sider Dayton and Donald Dayton, "Women in the Holiness Movement," originally presented in a seminar at the 1974 Christian Holiness Association convention, retrieved 8/21/23 from The Wesleyan Church Department of Education and Clergy Development: Women in Ministry Leadership, https://www.wesleyan.org/ecd/women-ministry-leadership, p.1.

12. Maxine Haines and Lee M. Haines, *Celebrate Our Daughters: 150 Years of Women in Wesleyan Ministry* (Indianapolis: Wesleyan Publishing House, 2004), p. 326.

13. Dr. J. Gaile Smith, "Equipping Women for Leadership in a Wesleyan Church," *Asbury Theological Seminary*, 2003, https://place.asburyseminary.edu/cgi/viewcontent.cgi?-referer=&httpsredir=1&article=1187&context=ecommonsatsdissertations.

Chapter Six - Dissecting Resistance to Kingdom **Fullness**

1. Episcopal Church. *The Book of Common Prayer and Administration of the Sacraments and Other Rites and Ceremonies of the Church: Together with the Psalter or Psalms of David According to the Use of the Episcopal Church.* New York: Seabury Press, 1979.

2. Dr. Lee M. Haines, "Recruiting/Deploying Women in Ministry in The Wesleyan Church," delivered on behalf of

the Board of General Superintendents at the Leadership Summit in December 1998. Women in Ministry Leadership, The Wesleyan Church, retrieved 8/8/23, https://cdn. resources.wesleyan.org/wesleyanrc/wp-content/uploads/ Recruiting-Deploying-Women-in-Ministry.pdf.

3. Karen Bates, "What We're Missing When Multiethnic Women Are Absent from Pastoral Staffs," Wesleyan Accent, June 5, 2017, https://wesleyanaccent.com/ karen-bates-missing-multiethnic-women-pastoral-staff/.

Chapter Seven - Living Surrendered

Chapter Eight - How We Steward Kingdom-Full Vocation

1. Interview, Rev. Dr. Tammy Dunahoo.

Chapter Nine - Do No Harm: Healthy, Practical Alternatives to the BGR

1. *Book of Common Prayer* Eucharist Rite II Confession of Sin

2. See *Just As I Am*, Billy Graham, Harper San Francisco, 1999.

3. "Five Essential Soft Skills to Develop in Any Job," Marlo Lyons, *Harvard Business Review*, February 28, 2023 https://hbr. org/2023/02/5-essential-soft-skills-to-develop-in-any-job

4. Aaron Earls, "The Church Growth Gap: The Big Get Bigger While the Small Get Smaller," *Christianity Today*, 2019 https://www.christianitytoday.com/news/2019/march/ lifeway-research-church-growth-attendance-size.html

5. Dr. Jo Anne Lyon

6. Dr. Andrea Summers, "3 Key Aspects of Mentoring Across the Gender Gap for the Sake of Mission," *Missio Alliance*, 2018

https://www.missioalliance.org/3-key-aspects-of-mentoring-across-the-gender-gap-for-the-sake-of-mission/

7. From a presentation given by Dr. Jo Anne Lyon

8. From a presentation given by Dr. Jo Anne Lyon

9. Paraphrasing Edward B. Pusey's translation of Confessions of St. Augustine, 1.1, *Christian Classics Ethereal Library* https://ccel.org/ccel/augustine/confess/confess.ii.i.html#ii.i-p0.2

10. Ron Dixon, "The Billy Graham Rule's Unintended Consequences," *Outreach* magazine, October 13 2021, https://outreachmagazine.com/resources/books/christian-living-books/69362-the-billy-graham-rules-unintended-consequences.html

11. From a presentation given by Dr. Jo Anne Lyon

12. Dr. Jo Anne Lyon

13. Dr. Jo Anne Lyon

Chapter Ten - Side by Side: Co-Laboring Joyfully in the Fullness of the Holy Spirit

1. Tom McCall, "Asbury Professor: We're Witnessing a 'Surprising Work of God'" www.christianitytoday.com, *Christianity Today*, February 13, 2023, https://www.christianitytoday.com/ct/2023/february-web-only/asbury-revival-1970-2023-methodist-christian-holy-spirit.html

2. Daniel Silliman, "'No Celebrity Except Jesus': How Asbury Protected the Revival" www.christianitytoday.com, *Christianity Today*, February 23, 2023, https://www.christianitytoday.com/news/2023/february/asbury-revival-outpouring-protect-work-admin-volunteers.html

Chapter Eleven - Trust: How to Enter Hard Conversations & Listen for the Holy Spirit

1. The word "feminist" is simply someone who believes in the equality of women. In the American context, sometimes it is used with an additional load of assumptions and cultural and political connotations, then deployed as a kind of insult to dismiss leaders who are women. Historically, however, Wesleyan Methodist denominations were home to some of the early pioneers who worked for equal rights for women, like the right to own property and vote. The website for my own denomination explains: "From its beginnings, The Wesleyan Church has championed the equality of women both in society and in God's redemptive plan for mankind. In July of 1848, the first Women's Rights Convention was held in Seneca Falls, NY at the Wesleyan Methodist Chapel." *Women in Ministry Historical View*, Women in Ministry: Education and Clergy Development, retrieved May 2023, www.wesleyan.org/ecd/women-ministry-leadership.

Chapter Twelve - A Beautiful Vision: How Good It Can Be

1. Sarah A. Cooke, *Wayside Sketches: The Handmaiden of the Lord*, Chicago: T.B. Arnold, Publisher, 1896; Digital Edition 8/13/2002 by Holiness Data Ministry, http://wesley.nnu.edu/wesleyctr/books/2201-2300/HDM2219.pdf

Conclusion - The Body Anointed: Running the Race